How Cars WORK

Tom Newton

BLACK APPLE PRESS ★ A DIVISION OF NLC

www.howcarswork.com

Published by BLACK APPLE PRESS

a division of THE NEWTON LEARNING CENTER

1609 Fern Place

Vallejo, CA 94590

Library of Congress Catalog Number: 98-96784

ISBN 0-9668623-0-9

Twenty-fourth Edition

Printed in U.S.A by Gorham Printing

How Cars Work

- Explains the fundamentals of auto mechanics
- Describes the 250 most important car parts and how they work
- Contains 96 pages divided into seven chapters, an index, and a glossary
- Uses a "one topic per page" format

Each Chapter:

- Describes a major automotive system
- Begins with the general view, then discusses specific parts
- Has a test at the end

Each Page:

- Describes a single topic, part, or system of parts
- Has an illustration to identify and locate topic parts
- Has text to explain how it all works

How Cars Work:

- Gives the reader a general understanding of mechanical devices
- Allows a reader to better use auto motive workshop manuals
- Prepares a reader for beginning do-it-yourself car projects
- Equips the reader for intelligently solving car problems

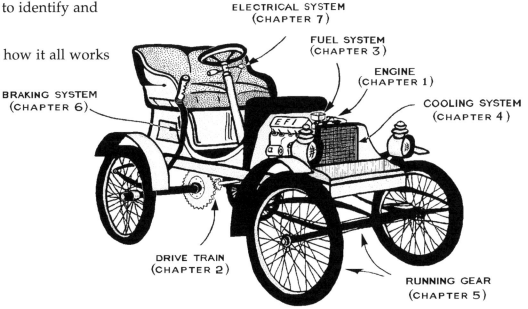

ELECTRICAL SYSTEM
(CHAPTER 7)

FUEL SYSTEM
(CHAPTER 3)

ENGINE
(CHAPTER 1)

COOLING SYSTEM
(CHAPTER 4)

BRAKING SYSTEM
(CHAPTER 6)

DRIVE TRAIN
(CHAPTER 2)

RUNNING GEAR
(CHAPTER 5)

TABLE OF CONTENTS

CHAPTER ONE

Engine

This chapter explains how automobile engines work. The illustration below shows the basic parts of a "V-8" *internal combustion* engine. Internal combustion means fuel burns inside an engine, in *combustion chambers*. Other types include the steam engine and the jet engine. Although there are many designs, the parts shown below are used in almost all automobile engines.

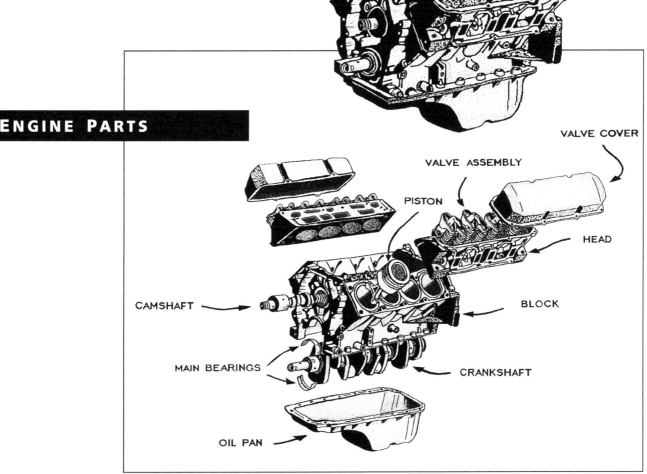

ENGINE PARTS

VALVE COVER

VALVE ASSEMBLY

PISTON

HEAD

CAMSHAFT

BLOCK

MAIN BEARINGS

CRANKSHAFT

OIL PAN

Combustion Chamber

Fuel burns in *combustion chambers* inside an engine. The walls and ceilings of these chambers are hollowed into an engine *head*. The floor of a combustion chamber is also the top of a *piston*, which moves up and down as an engine runs. One combustion chamber is directly above each *cylinder*, with a piston sliding in each cylinder. The explosive force created inside a combustion chamber pushes a piston down, creating the motion which moves a car.

As an engine runs, pistons pump up and down, one after another, in a carefully-arranged order. This up and down movement changes to spinning motion by the action of a *crankshaft*. The spin motion, or *angular momentum*, then rotates the wheels.

An automobile engine really has just one job—to create spinning motion.

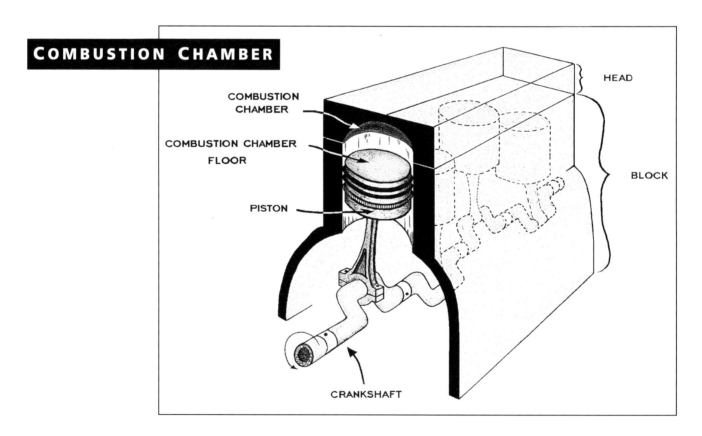

COMBUSTION CHAMBER

COMBUSTION CHAMBER

COMBUSTION CHAMBER FLOOR

PISTON

CRANKSHAFT

HEAD

BLOCK

Block

An engine *block* is the most basic part of an engine. A block is a large casting of iron or aluminum with small passageways for oil and water circulation. A block itself, however, has no moving parts.

Several large holes or tubes, called *cylinders,* are built into each engine block. Pistons slide up and down in these cylinders and each engine will have the same number of cylinders, pistons, and combustion chambers. Automobile engines usually have four, six, or eight cylinders commonly arranged in either a straight line or a "V" shape (shown below).

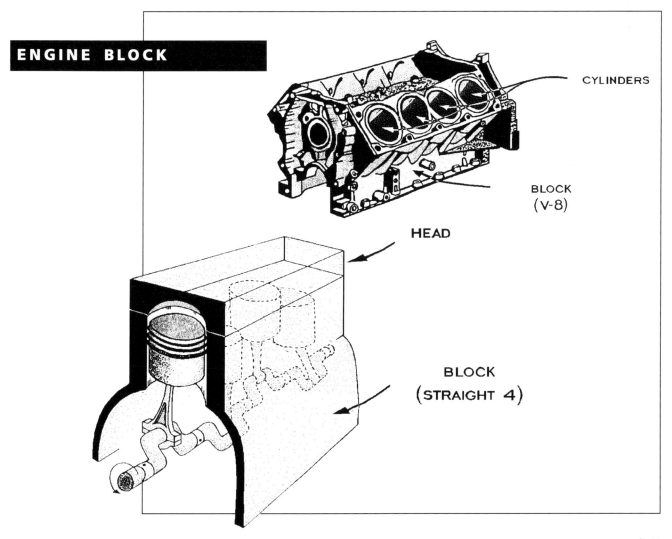

ENGINE BLOCK

CYLINDERS

BLOCK
(V-8)

HEAD

BLOCK
(STRAIGHT 4)

Crankshaft

A *crankshaft* changes the pumping motion of the pistons into spinning motion. A crankshaft also has smooth surfaces for connecting to a block and tiny passageways inside for delivering lubricating oil. *Balancing lobes* are used as counterweights to balance a crankshaft and prevent damage from wobbling.

A crankshaft fits lengthwise to the underside of an engine block, extending through that block at each end. At the front of an engine, rubber drive belts attach to the end of a crankshaft to deliver power to other car accessories. At the rear of a block, *drive train* parts attach to the crankshaft-end and transfer power to the wheels.

Oil seals prevent oil leaks where a crankshaft extends through a block. These rubber "O-rings" fit around the end of a crankshaft to prevent oil from leaking out, even while a crankshaft turns.

An *oil pan* covers and protects a crankshaft from road dirt and moisture. The area inside an oil pan is called the *crankcase* and holds the engine oil. An oil pan also encloses an *oil pump* which is usually bolted to the bottom of an engine where it can extend to the very bottom of a crankcase. An *oil plug* or *oil drain bolt* is threaded into the bottom of an oil pan to drain engine oil.

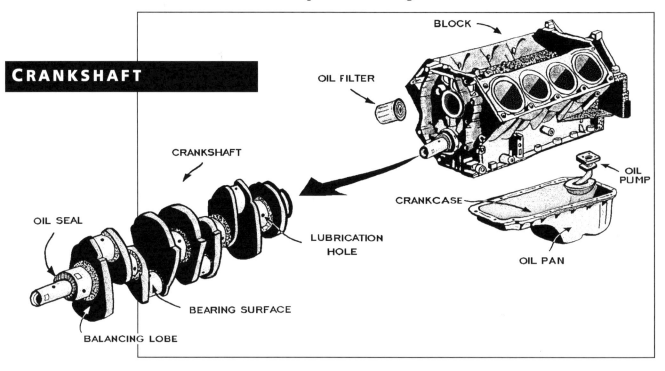

CRANKSHAFT

BLOCK

OIL FILTER

OIL PUMP

CRANKCASE

OIL PAN

CRANKSHAFT

LUBRICATION HOLE

OIL SEAL

BEARING SURFACE

BALANCING LOBE

Main Bearings

*M*ain *bearings* are smooth semi-circular metal straps which provide a smooth surface for the motion between a crankshaft and a block. Five or more main bearing sets hold a crankshaft in place. A heavy crankshaft must rotate fast and yet be held tightly to the block. The main bearings do this by providing a polished surface to reduce friction and a perfect fit to eliminate wobble.

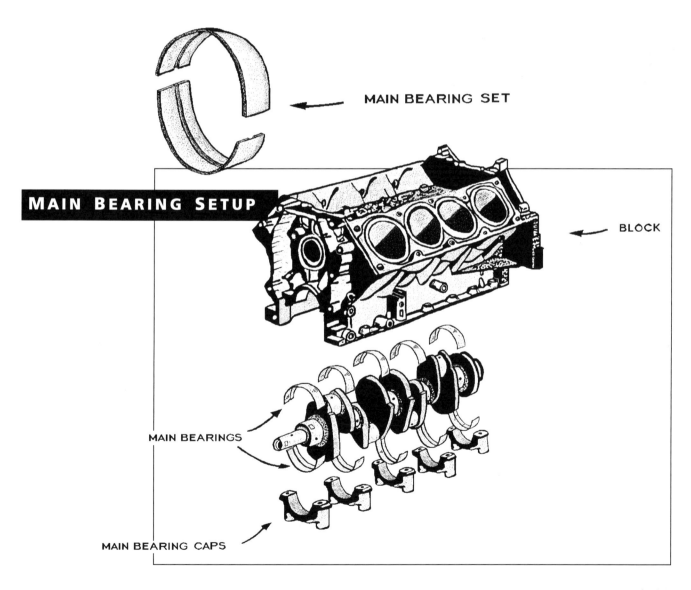

MAIN BEARING SET

MAIN BEARING SETUP

BLOCK

MAIN BEARINGS

MAIN BEARING CAPS

Piston

A *piston* resembles an empty soup can turned upside down. When fuel ignites, the explosive force pushes a piston down with bullet-like power. Each piston attaches to the crankshaft with a *connecting rod,* commonly called a *con rod.* A connecting rod attaches to the crankshaft in the same way a crankshaft connects to a block, with highly polished circular strap bearings. These bearings are called *connecting rod bearings, con rod bearings,* or simply *rod bearings.* A piston attaches to a connecting rod with a *piston pin,* also called a *wrist pin.*

The alignment between a crankshaft and piston must be slightly off-center to direct the strong downward force a little to one side. If the force of a piston rushing downwards hit a crankshaft squarely, something would break.

Interestingly, the attachment hole for a piston pin causes a piston to expand unevenly as an engine heats. A piston is consequently built in an oval shape. When heated to proper running temperature a piston expands to a circular shape, matching the engine cylinder. This is one reason why an automobile engine must reach proper operating temperature to run properly.

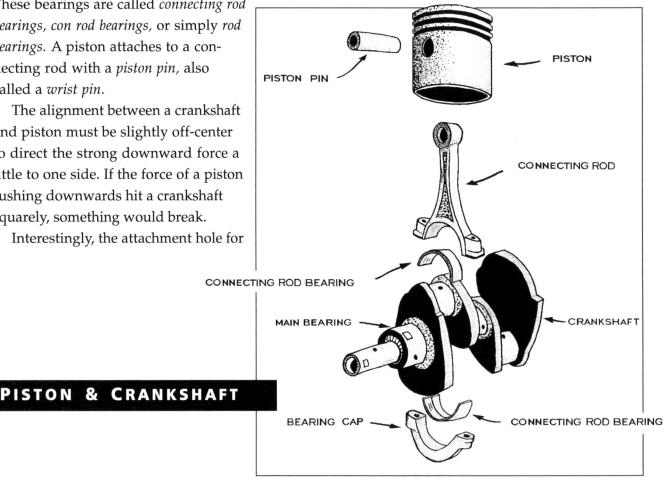

PISTON PIN

PISTON

CONNECTING ROD

CONNECTING ROD BEARING

MAIN BEARING

CRANKSHAFT

BEARING CAP

CONNECTING ROD BEARING

PISTON & CRANKSHAFT

Rings

Rings are like steel bracelets that fit in grooves around each piston. A set of three or four individual rings usually encircles each piston. Although pistons slide up and down in cylinders, they never actually touch the cylinder walls; only the rings touch the walls.

The upper rings or *compression rings* press outward against the wall of a cylinder to provide a seal strong enough to contain the explosive burning inside a combustion chamber. The lower ring or *oil ring* prevents oil in the crankcase from splashing and seeping into a combustion chamber from below. Oil rings wipe excess oil down from cylinder walls and back into a crankcase.

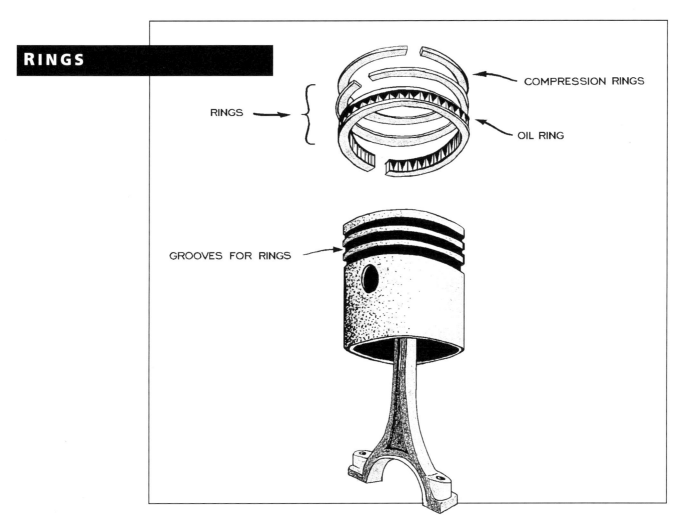

RINGS

RINGS →

COMPRESSION RINGS

OIL RING

GROOVES FOR RINGS →

Camshaft

A *camshaft* is the mechanical brain of an engine, responsible for coordinating all the major parts. A camshaft uses egg-shaped *lobes* to control the *timing* of the opening and closing of engine *valves* which regulate the flow of fuel through an engine.

A camshaft looks similar to a crankshaft and may be located directly above a crankshaft, inside an engine block (shown below), or on top of an engine head, as in the *overhead camshaft* design (shown on page 17).

When an overhead camshaft is used in a "V"shaped engine, two separate camshafts are often used. This arrangement is called a *double overhead camshaft* (dohc).

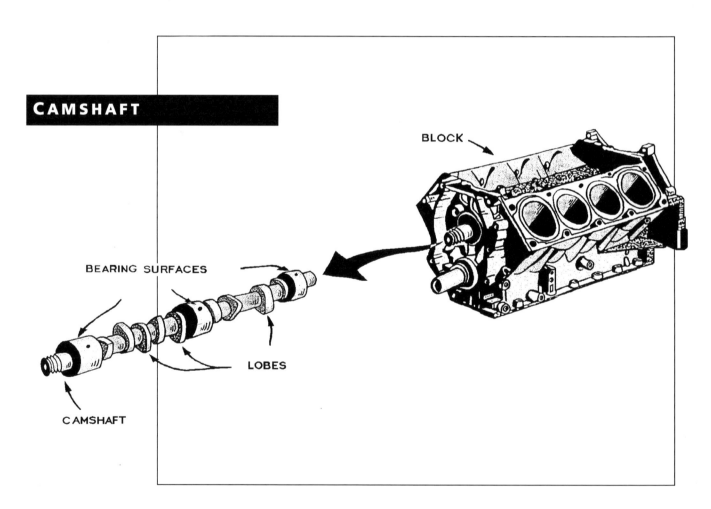

CAMSHAFT

BLOCK

BEARING SURFACES

LOBES

CAMSHAFT

Timing Systems

A *timing chain* or *timing belt* connects a camshaft and a crankshaft, holding them in the same relative position to each other at all times. Older models used a direct gear to gear connection. *Timing marks* stamped into the two gears must be aligned to insure correct assembly. If a timing chain or belt skips just one gear *cog,* an engine will not work. A camshaft and crankshaft must always be positioned correctly to coordinate the workings of an engine. This coordination is part of the *timing* of an engine.

TIMING CHAIN

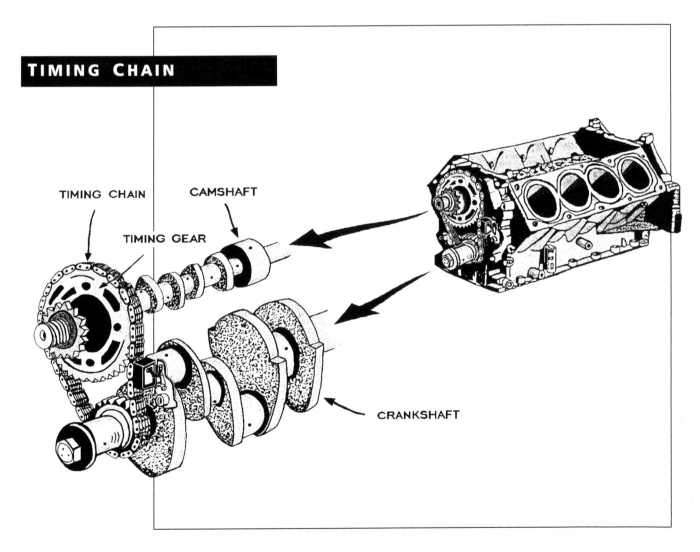

TIMING CHAIN

TIMING GEAR

CAMSHAFT

CRANKSHAFT

Head

A *head* or *cylinder head* is a solid metal piece that fits on top of an engine block. Rounded indentations in a head provide space for the combustion chambers. A head also serves as the foundation for a *valve assembly*. A head also provides the openings where combustion chambers receive and discharge gasoline fumes and a threaded hole into each combustion chamber for a *sparkplug*. Two separate heads are used with a "V" shaped block, one for each side of the "V."

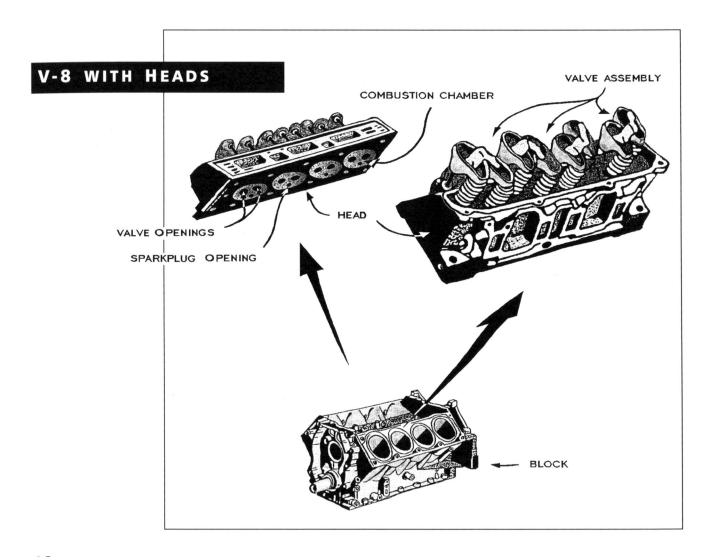

V-8 WITH HEADS

COMBUSTION CHAMBER

VALVE ASSEMBLY

VALVE OPENINGS

SPARKPLUG OPENING

HEAD

BLOCK

Valves

Engine *valves* are doors to the combustion chambers. An engine has at least two valves for each combustion chamber, one that opens to let the fuel mixture enter, called the *intake valve,* and another, the *exhaust valve,* to allow the exhaust fumes to be pushed out. Valves fit through a head in carefully-drilled holes. A *valve guide* provides a good seal and a smooth sliding surface for a *valve stem.*

Valves are controlled by a camshaft.

With the overhead camshaft system (shown below), a camshaft is located above an engine head. The lobes of a camshaft push open the valves; strong springs push them closed. The shape of the lobes determines when, how far, and how long a valve will open. When closed, valves fit perfectly in their seats, sealing the combustion chambers. Valves rotate slightly each time they open to distribute wear evenly on the surfaces that touch.

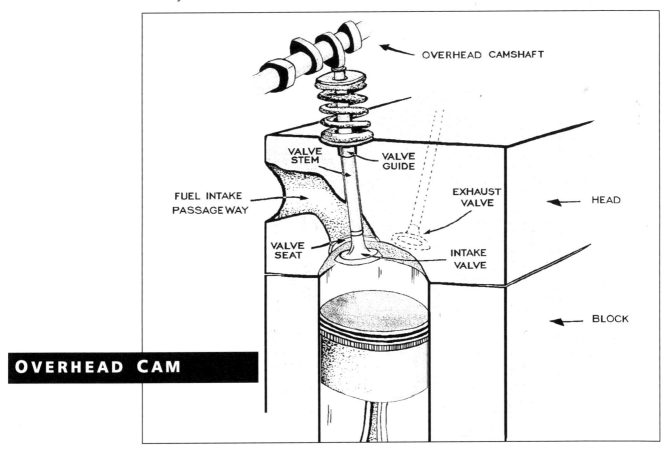

OVERHEAD CAM

OVERHEAD CAMSHAFT

VALVE STEM

VALVE GUIDE

FUEL INTAKE PASSAGEWAY

EXHAUST VALVE

HEAD

VALVE SEAT

INTAKE VALVE

BLOCK

Valve Assembly

A *valve assembly*, also called a *rocker arm assembly* or *valve train*, includes the parts that create contact between a valve and the camshaft lobes and the parts that hold and guide all the valves. A *push rod valve assembly* is shown below. Here the camshaft is located in an engine block and long *push rods* extend through a head to push *rocker arms* that, in turn, push open the valves. *Valve return springs* hold the valves closed.

New valve assembly designs include *Variable Valve Timing* and *Electronic Lift Control* systems where complex cone shaped lobes are electronically positioned to increase engine efficiency.

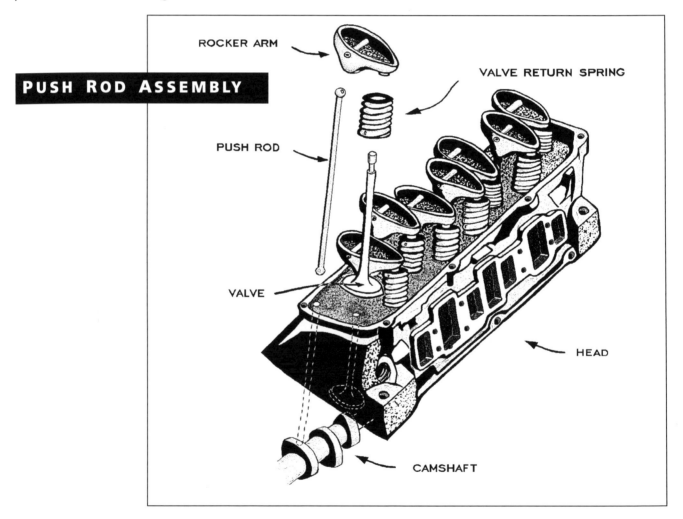

PUSH ROD ASSEMBLY

ROCKER ARM

VALVE RETURN SPRING

PUSH ROD

VALVE

HEAD

CAMSHAFT

ENGINE TEST

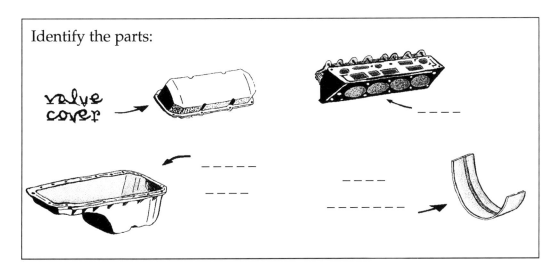

Identify the parts:

valve cover →

1. Fuel is burned in _____, inside an engine. *(Answer on p. 8)*

2. What does dohc stand for? *(p. 14)*
   _____

3. The top of a piston is also the _____ of a combustion chamber. *(p. 8)*

4. A camshaft controls the opening and closing of _____. *(p. 14)*

5. Angular momentum is the technical name for _____. *(p. 8)*

6. Why is the alignment between a crankshaft and a piston slightly off-center? *(p. 12)*
   _____
   _____

7. The lobes of a camshaft are egg shaped. (T) (F) *(p. 14)*

8. Engine valves are like _____ to the combustion chambers. *(p. 17)*

9. Rings never touch the walls of a cylinder. (T) (F) *(p. 13)*

10. A timing chain connects a _____ _____ and a _____. *(p. 15)*

11. Why is a piston manufactured in an oval shape when it slides in a circular cylinder? *(p. 12)* _____

12. Bearings are used to _____
    (p. 11)

13. Steam and jet engines are examples of _____ combustion engines. *(p. 7)*

14. Why is the total number of cylinders in an engine usually an even number?
    _____

CHAPTER TWO

Drive Train

A *drive train* includes the many parts that transfer spinning motion from an engine to the wheels. A drive train begins at the rear of an engine, connecting to a crankshaft where it extends through a block. This connection must engage and disengage quickly, smoothly, and with enough force to move a car fast.

A drive train has three jobs:
1. Transferring spin force from an engine to the wheels
2. Changing the rate of spin delivered to the wheels by shifting gears
3. Connecting and disconnecting an engine from the wheels in order to start or idle

There are many drive train arrangements used to accomplish these tasks including full-time four wheel drive systems and the new variable speed transmissions. The next two pages will cover the two most common types of drive trains: *rear wheel drive* and *front wheel drive.*

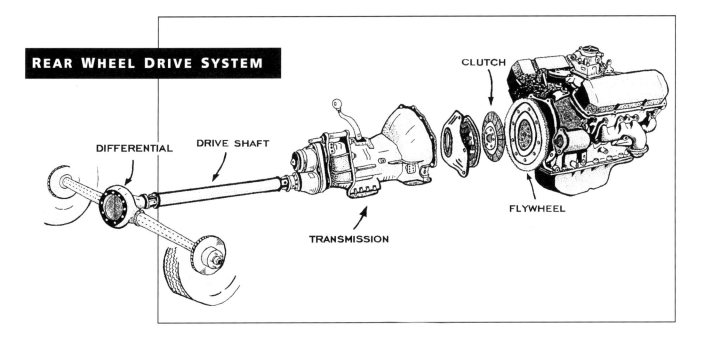

REAR WHEEL DRIVE SYSTEM

DIFFERENTIAL

DRIVE SHAFT

TRANSMISSION

CLUTCH

FLYWHEEL

Rear Wheel Drive

In the conventional *rear wheel drive* system an engine is in the front of a vehicle. A *transmission* connects to the rear of the engine and a *drive shaft* connects to the rear of the transmission to extend the spin motion to a *differential*. A differential transfers the spin motion to the axle shaft which connects to the rear wheels. In most cars only one wheel receives spin power at a time. Almost all possibilities of engine placement and drive train design are used, with emphasis on placing weight over the drive wheels, saving space, and providing balanced cornering.

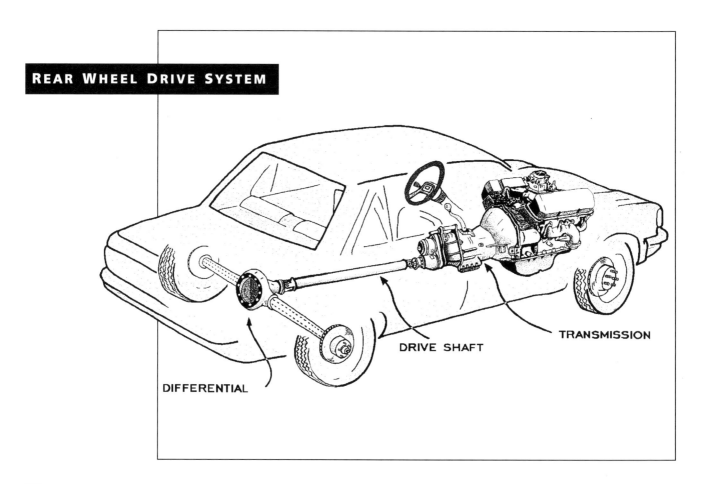

REAR WHEEL DRIVE SYSTEM

DIFFERENTIAL

DRIVE SHAFT

TRANSMISSION

Front Wheel Drive

In the *front wheel drive* system all the parts necessary to transfer force to the wheels are in the front of the vehicle. With this arrangement a front wheel receives the spin power. This complicates matters because now the front wheels must receive the powerful spin force from an engine, plus turn right and left, and move up and down.

Front wheel drive systems often place an engine sideways in the engine compartment. This arrangement is called a *transverse* engine placement. Sideways placement saves space and eliminates the need for a separate differential and long *drive shaft*; here the crankshaft is aimed directly at the wheel assembly. A *transaxle* is often used in the front wheel drive arrangement as a combination transmission and differential.

Four wheel drive (FWD) is a third drive train variation combining rear and front wheel drive systems. With FWD, used on most sports utility vehicles (SUV), all four wheels receive spin power when needed for slippery conditions. Many manufacturers have introduced full time FWD drive or all wheel drive (AWD) systems, where computers monitor slipping wheels and automatically deliver the best drive wheel combinations for the conditions.

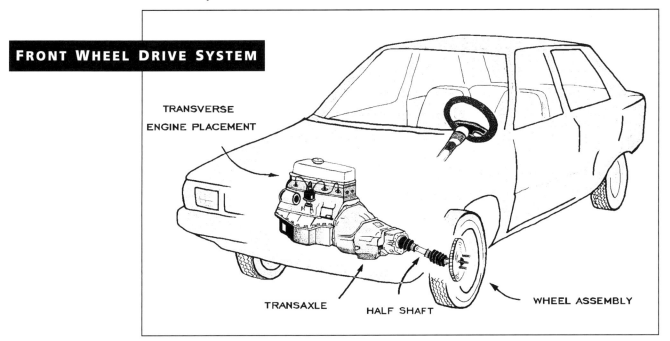

FRONT WHEEL DRIVE SYSTEM

TRANSVERSE ENGINE PLACEMENT

TRANSAXLE

HALF SHAFT

WHEEL ASSEMBLY

Transmission

A *transmission* provides another way to change car speed besides the gas pedal or brakes. A transmission uses different-sized gears to change the speed of rotation delivered to the wheels.

There are three types of transmissions:
1. Manual
2. Automatic
3. Continuously variable

With a *manual transmission*, often called a *stick shift*, the gears are changed by hand with the *gear shift lever*. This is done in conjunction with a clutch pedal. Spin force from an engine is transferred to a *mainshaft* and *drive gear*, which can be slid by hand along the *countershaft cluster gear* to change gear combinations. *Synchronizer* gears help slide one gear to another. Transmissions usually have from three to six different forward gears, each producing different speed/power combinations. Some transmissions are equipped with *overdrives* to provide an additional *high gear* for improving gas mileage during freeway driving. Big rig trucks often have 36 different gears.

An *automatic transmission* has automatic gear shifting and an automatic clutch mechanism as well. These transmissions feature a totally liquid connection to a crankshaft and in modern vehicles include the latest in electronic improvements.

A *continuously variable transmission* (CVT) provides automatic, seamless, shifting — gear shifting that cannot be felt. This new design is even mechanically simpler than a regular transmission. With another innovation, the *AutoShift* transmission, a driver can change between an automatic and manual transmission style while driving.

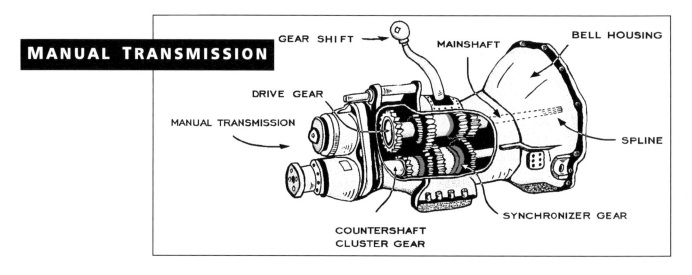

MANUAL TRANSMISSION

GEAR SHIFT

MAINSHAFT

BELL HOUSING

DRIVE GEAR

MANUAL TRANSMISSION

SPLINE

SYNCHRONIZER GEAR

COUNTERSHAFT
CLUSTER GEAR

Clutch

A *clutch* is always used with a manual transmission. Pushing in a *clutch pedal* separates the spinning part of an engine from the rest of a drive train allowing a driver to shift gears. This separation releases pressure on the gears, allowing them to slide easily from one gear combination to another. Separation of an engine from the rest of a drive train also provides a "neutral" position for starting and idling.

As a clutch pedal is eased-out, a *clutch disc* is slowly forced into contact with the spinning surface of a *flywheel*. Slipping and small vibrations occur at first and considerable heat is generated. With a clutch pedal all the way out, a clutch disc is pressed tight to a flywheel by the strong springs of a *pressure plate* and no slipping or clutch wear occurs;

the transfer of spin power is complete.

A flywheel is bolted to a crankshaft at the rear of an engine. The large size and weight of a flywheel helps absorb rattling and vibrations as a clutch disc makes contact. A flywheel also quiets engine vibrations.

When assembled, the *splined* mainshaft extends through the center of the pressure plate and *release bearing*, sliding perfectly into matching notches in the center of a clutch disc. The *splined* end of a mainshaft secures and centers a clutch disc, which has no other attachment. A release bearing, sometimes called a *throw-out bearing*, reduces wear on a pressure plate when a clutch pedal is pushed down. A *bell housing* encloses all these parts to protect them from moisture and dirt.

CLUTCH

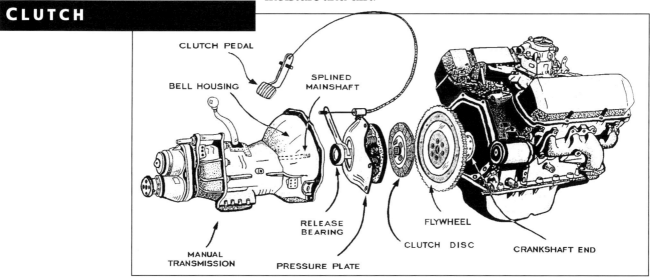

CLUTCH PEDAL
BELL HOUSING
SPLINED MAINSHAFT
MANUAL TRANSMISSION
RELEASE BEARING
PRESSURE PLATE
FLYWHEEL
CLUTCH DISC
CRANKSHAFT END

Torque Converter

A *torque converter* serves as a clutch for an automatic transmission. With a torque converter there is no mechanical connection between an engine and drive train, no solid clutch disc. Instead, a torque converter uses a liquid connection to transfer spin force. With a torque converter the viscosity and kinetic energy of a liquid is used to transfer the spinning power of an engine to a drive train.

This concept can be demonstrated by placing two household fans facing each other. If only one is switched on, the other will soon spin at a similar rate. A torque converter uses this concept but employs liquid instead of air to make a stronger, more reliable connection. The liquid, called *transmission fluid*, also serves as a lubricant for all the moving parts in an automatic transmission.

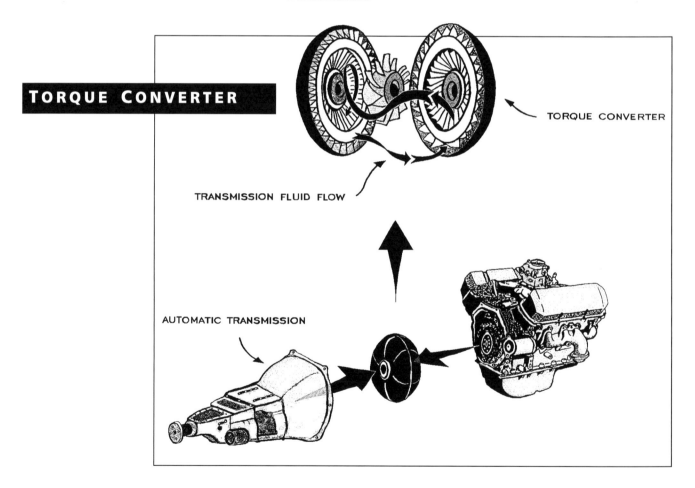

TORQUE CONVERTER

TORQUE CONVERTER

TRANSMISSION FLUID FLOW

AUTOMATIC TRANSMISSION

Universal Joints

Universal joints, usually called *U-joints*, transfer spinning power through the changing angles from road bumps and the sway caused by steering around corners. The transfer of engine power must be smooth and continuous, despite these constantly changing angles. U-joints attach to each end of a drive shaft. U-joints are also used in some steering systems and in other automotive applications.

Because of the wider range of movement required by front wheel drive wheel assemblies, stronger, more flexible U-joint design is required. These U-joints, called *constant velocity joints* or *CV-joints*, use ball bearing mechanisms to reduce friction and provide the extra strength required to handle the complex forces and movements used in front wheel drive designs.

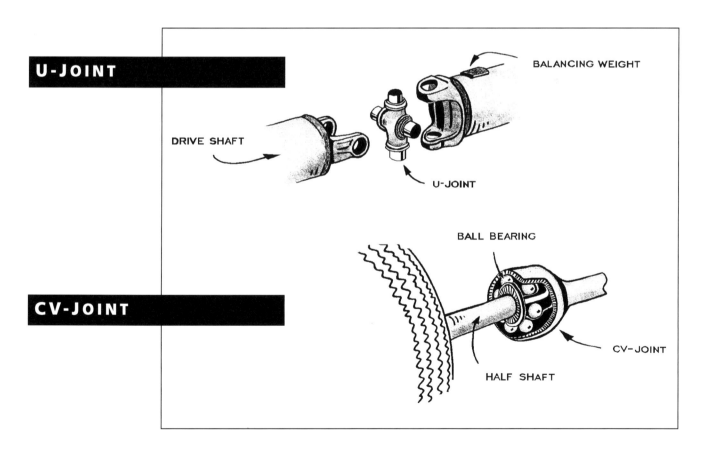

U-JOINT

BALANCING WEIGHT

DRIVE SHAFT

U-JOINT

CV-JOINT

BALL BEARING

CV-JOINT

HALF SHAFT

Drive Shaft

A *drive shaft* is a steel tube. In a rear wheel drive car, a drive shaft extends from the transmission to a differential with U-joints attached at each end. Small dents, or even mud, can affect the surprisingly delicate balance required. To avoid the balance sensitivity inherent in a long shaft, two short drive shafts are sometimes used instead, requiring an additional U-joint in the middle.

In a front wheel drive vehicle, *half shafts* are used in place of a long drive shaft. A half shaft is a short steel rod that connects a wheel assembly to a transaxle using CV-joints to make the connections. CV-joint assemblies are easily damaged by moisture or dirt and are protected by rubber "boots."

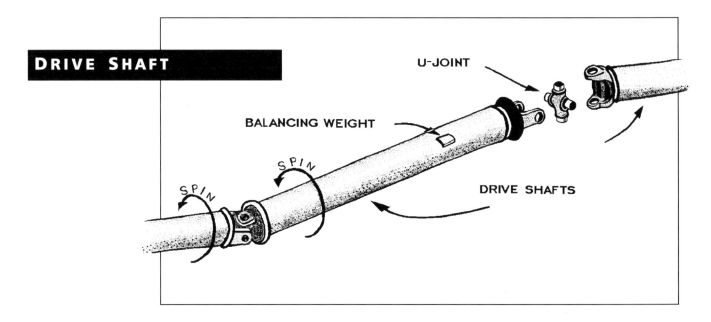

DRIVE SHAFT

U-JOINT

BALANCING WEIGHT

SPIN

SPIN

DRIVE SHAFTS

Differential

A *differential* is a watermelon-size part located between the two rear wheels. A differential is only used in rear wheel drive vehicles and contains the gears necessary to transfer spin force around a corner as well as mechanisms for several other important tasks. A differential has hollow arms extending to each rear *wheel assembly*. These arms enclose the *axles* which connect the wheels with the main rotating gears in a differential (shown below).

In most cars, only one wheel actually receives power, the *drive wheel*. This is adequate for most road surfaces, but in mud, sand, or snow a single drive wheel can easily slip, dig-in, and get stuck. A *limited slip differential* or *positraction* system helps eliminate this problem by automatically transferring power from a slipping drive wheel to the opposite wheel, doubling the chances of getting good traction.

A differential also allows the two rear wheels to rotate at different speeds. For example, when a car goes around a corner the outside wheels travel a slightly greater distance than the inside wheels, and the outside wheels must spin slightly faster to compensate. If a solid connection between both wheels remained, and they rotated at different speeds, something would break. A differential eliminates this problem.

A front wheel drive vehicle uses a special differential called a *transaxle*. A transaxle is a combination differential/transmission.

A four wheel drive (FWD) vehicle has two differentials to supply power to all four wheels. Here a *transfer case* serves as a second differential for the front two wheels.

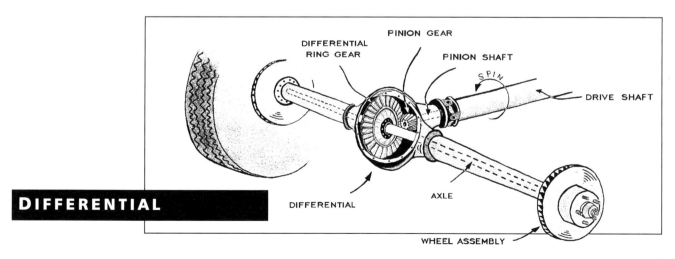

DIFFERENTIAL

DIFFERENTIAL RING GEAR · PINION GEAR · PINION SHAFT · SPIN · DRIVE SHAFT · DIFFERENTIAL · AXLE · WHEEL ASSEMBLY

DRIVE TRAIN TEST

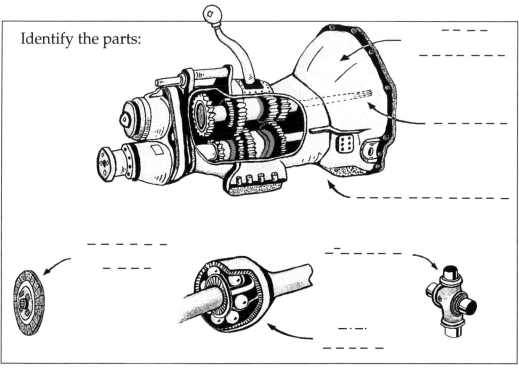

Identify the parts:

1. Automatic transmission lubricant is called_____. *(p. 26)*

2. CV-joints are protected from dirt and moisture by_____. *(p. 28)*

3. Why is a flywheel heavy? _____*(p. 25)*

4. An engine mounted sideways is called a _____engine placement. *(p. 23)*

5. _____ are used in place of drive shafts in front wheel drive vehicles. *(p. 28)*

6.   Manual transmission: clutch automatic transmission : _____ *(p. 26)*

7. Automobile wheels rotate at different speeds when cornering. (T) (F) *(p. 29)*

8. A _____connects a transmission to a differential. (p. 28)

9. A small_____ gear turns a large differential _____gear. *(p. 29)*

10._____gears help to smoothly slide one gear to another. *(p. 24)*

11. A clutch disconnects an engine from a drive train by separating a clutch disc from a _____ *(p. 25)*

12. A drive train changes car speed by switching_____combinations. *(p. 21 & 24)*

CHAPTER THREE

Fuel System

A fuel system has three basic jobs:

1. To supply an engine with fuel
2. To mix this fuel continuously with air in varying combinations
3. To discharge the burned remains safely

At top speed, the flow of air rushing through an engine approaches the speed of sound. Gasoline droplets are mixed into this air-flow as it enters an engine. The *air/fuel mixture* then burns in the combustion chambers, and the exhaust is blown out the tail pipe.

The air-flow through an engine is created by the action of the pistons moving up and down. As pistons move downwards, they create a partial vacuum which immediately pulls in the air/fuel mixture. After the mixture ignites and a piston is driven down, it moves up again to push the burned remains out. The opening and closing of the engine valves directs the air/fuel mixture through an engine and into the exhaust pipe.

A fuel system uses either a *carburetor* or *fuel injectors* to mix and deliver fuel.

THE FUEL SYSTEM

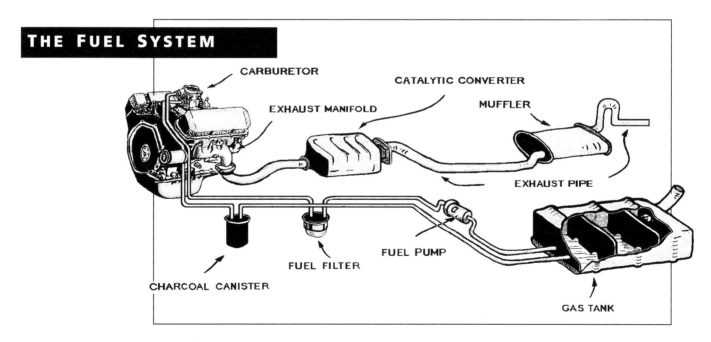

CARBURETOR

CATALYTIC CONVERTER

EXHAUST MANIFOLD

MUFFLER

EXHAUST PIPE

CHARCOAL CANISTER

FUEL FILTER

FUEL PUMP

GAS TANK

Carburetor

A *carburetor* controls the amount and mixture of fuel delivered to an engine. A *throttle valve* or *butterfly valve* regulates fuel volume. When a gas pedal is pushed down, a throttle valve correspondingly swings open, introducing more fuel into the air-flow. This increases engine revolutions and car speed.

A carburetor must continuously adjust the air/fuel mixture to create the most explosive combination possible inside a combustion chamber. The *choke plate* illustrated below is shown in half-open position. In this position, air entering the carburetor *throat* is partially blocked, causing less air to enter the air/fuel mixture. This mixture, rich in gasoline, is necessary for a cold engine to operate properly. As an engine warms, an *automatic choke* slowly moves a choke plate to a more open or straight-up position, automatically adjusting the air/fuel mixture.

At full throttle, the air-flow is funneled through a carburetor at great velocities. Droplets of liquid gasoline are automatically drawn from a fuel *bowl* into this air-flow by the force of the moving air. When the droplets hit the air-flow they *atomize* or break into very small particles. This air/fuel mixture enters an *intake manifold* and is then sucked into individual combustion chambers through the intake valve openings. Once in the combustion chambers, the air/fuel mixture is compressed, exploded, and the waste pushed out through the exhaust valve openings and exhaust pipe.

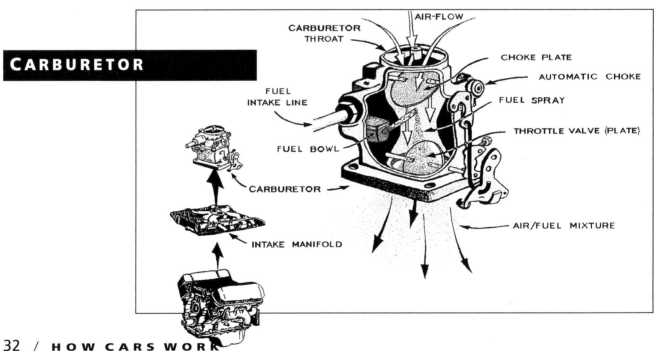

CARBURETOR

AIR-FLOW
CARBURETOR THROAT
CHOKE PLATE
AUTOMATIC CHOKE
FUEL INTAKE LINE
FUEL SPRAY
THROTTLE VALVE (PLATE)
FUEL BOWL
CARBURETOR
AIR/FUEL MIXTURE
INTAKE MANIFOLD

Fuel Injection

Fuel injection systems spray gasoline into the air-flow, rather than having fuel droplets drawn-in automatically, as with a carburetor. A spray system is a more precise, controllable, and efficient fuel delivery system, yielding greater economy and cleaner burning.

There are three main types of fuel injection systems:

1. Direct fuel injection
2. Ported fuel injection
3. Throttle body fuel injection

Direct fuel injection uses a separate injector for each combustion chamber and represents the original design. These injectors screw into an engine head, extending into the combustion chambers, alongside the sparkplugs. A tiny gasoline pipe is connected to each injector and a control mechanism regulates the amount of spray.

Ported fuel injection (shown below) is a second generation injector system. This design also uses one injector for each combustion chamber, but the injectors do not spray directly into a combustion chamber. Here, an injector is in the intake manifold just outside each combustion chamber, in the "intake manifold port."

Throttle body fuel injection represents a third, more modern, and simplified injector system. Here, a single injector is positioned in a carburetor body and this injector acts as a more precise and controllable carburetor. Like a carburetor, a throttle body system directs atomized fuel into the air-flow for further mixture in an intake manifold.

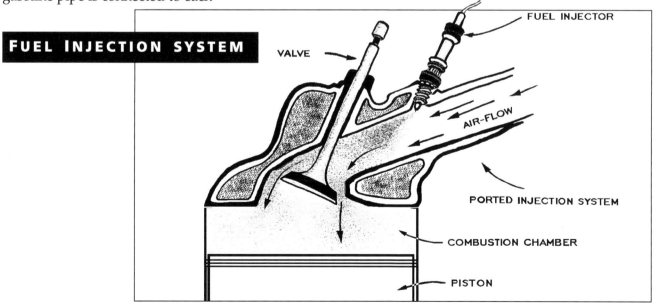

FUEL INJECTION SYSTEM

VALVE

FUEL INJECTOR

AIR-FLOW

PORTED INJECTION SYSTEM

COMBUSTION CHAMBER

PISTON

Computerized Fuel Injection

Computer controlled injector systems include *electronic fuel injection* (EFI), *digital electronic fuel injection* (DEFI), and more recently electronic *sequential multiport fuel injection* (SMPI). In these systems, a computer receives information from a variety of sensors strategically placed throughout a vehicle. Sensors and injectors are connected to a central computer, often termed *electronic control module* (ECM), *electronic engine control* (EEC), or *engine control unit* (ECU), depending on the manufacturer.

Common sensors include a manifold air pressure (MAP) sensor, plate sensor, pivoting flap sensor, manifold oxygen sensors, mass air-flow sensor, speed-density air sensor, barometric pressure (BARO) sensor, manifold air temperature (MAT) sensor, coolant temperature sensors, variable-resistance sensors, and crankshaft position sensors.

The main advantage of any injection system is the high degree of control over the fuel mixture. Depending on the computer analysis of sensor data, three variables can be used to control the amount of gasoline injected: the size of the spray nozzle, the length of spray time, and the spray pressure. These complex operations require computer control. As with most automotive computers, a system failure defaults to average settings, enabling vehicles to continue to operate.

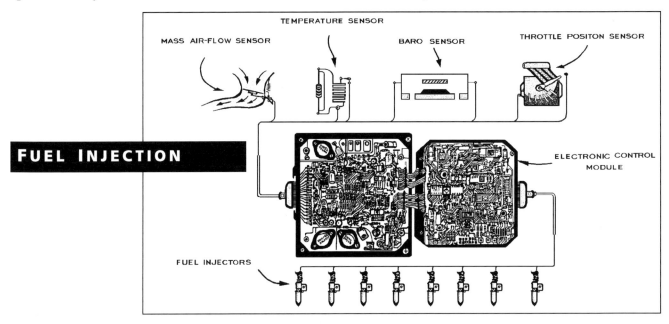

FUEL INJECTION

MASS AIR-FLOW SENSOR

TEMPERATURE SENSOR

BARO SENSOR

THROTTLE POSITON SENSOR

ELECTRONIC CONTROL MODULE

FUEL INJECTORS

Gasoline Tank

The primary purpose of a *gasoline tank* is to store gasoline, but tanks have other jobs as well. For example, a sensor system for the *dashboard fuel gauge*, often a plastic float, is built into most tanks. Gas tanks also have *baffle plates* inside to stop gasoline from sloshing during hard cornering, an electric submersible *transfer fuel pump* (shown below), a *water detector* sensor, and a filter for screening out large unwanted particles.

Gasoline tanks are also designed to prevent gasoline fumes from escaping into the atmosphere. Most vehicles use a *charcoal canister* (see page 31) or a *vapor holding canister* to trap fumes while allowing a free flow of air into a tank to equalize atmospheric pressure. Charcoal canisters are often located in an engine compartment and may also trap fuel-overflow from a carburetor, returning it to the tank.

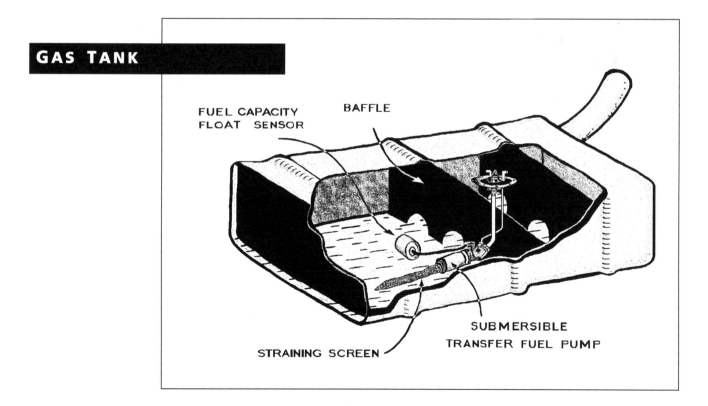

GAS TANK

FUEL CAPACITY FLOAT SENSOR

BAFFLE

STRAINING SCREEN

SUBMERSIBLE TRANSFER FUEL PUMP

Fuel Pump

Providing enough fuel for rapid acceleration is the main job of a *fuel pump*. When a driver steps on a gas pedal the feeling of seamless acceleration is the result of mechanical and electronic devices including several sophisticated fuel pumps and *pressure regulators*.

A variety of fuel pumps deliver fuel to engines, including: the in-line *electric fuel pump*, *mechanical diaphragm pump*, *precision fuel injector pump*, carburetor *accelerator pump*, and a submersible gasoline tank turbine *transfer pump* (shown on page 35).

Most vehicles use a transfer pump to deliver fuel from a gasoline tank to the top of an engine. With some fuel injection systems, fuel must be pumped through individual fuel injector nozzles using precise pumps on each injector. Most injector systems have a single injector pump that supplies fuel pressure for all injectors. Electric fuel pumps are used in fuel injection systems because they can deliver a very reliable fuel pressure. Electric pumps are usually rotary types, where an electric motor turns an internal paddle wheel or *impeller*.

Carbureted fuel systems often use *mechanical diaphragm* pumps mounted to an engine block. Mechanical pumps use engine parts to move a *power arm* and a thick rubber *diaphragm* back and forth, creating the pumping force.

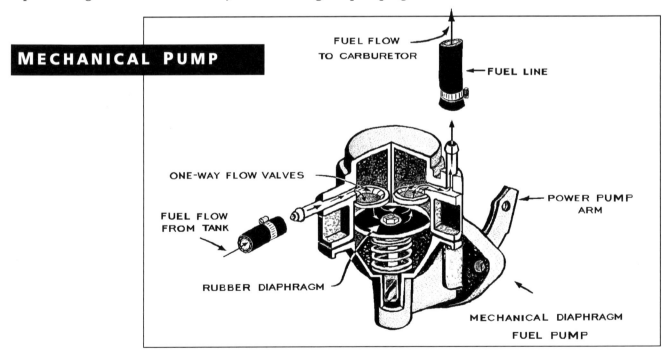

MECHANICAL PUMP

FUEL FLOW TO CARBURETOR

FUEL LINE

ONE-WAY FLOW VALVES

FUEL FLOW FROM TANK

POWER PUMP ARM

RUBBER DIAPHRAGM

MECHANICAL DIAPHRAGM FUEL PUMP

Air & Fuel Filters

Air filters trap dirt particles before they enter an engine. Without an air filter, dirt from the atmosphere would contaminate the sensitive air/fuel mixture and possibly clog the small passageways in a fuel system. Air filters are usually located on top of an engine and all air taken into an engine must pass through these filters. Filters are usually made of pleated paper and fine mesh screen. An air filter will clean about 10,000 gallons of air for every gallon of fuel burned.

Fuel filters trap unwanted particles, water, and other contaminants in the fuel before they enter a fuel pump, carburetor, or fuel injector. There are many types and locations for fuel filters.

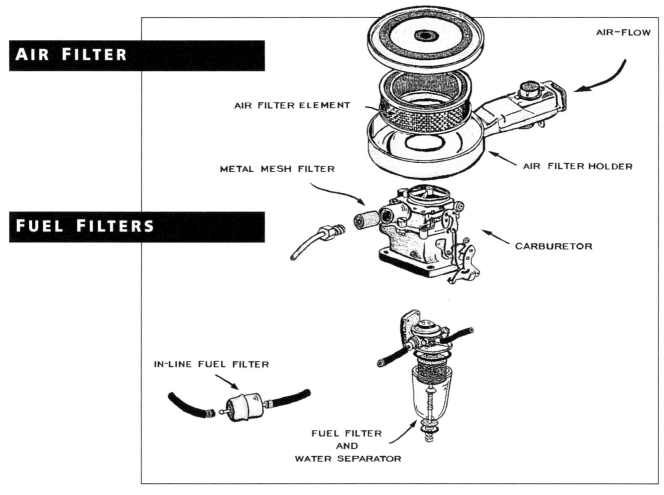

AIR FILTER

AIR-FLOW

AIR FILTER ELEMENT

AIR FILTER HOLDER

METAL MESH FILTER

FUEL FILTERS

CARBURETOR

IN-LINE FUEL FILTER

FUEL FILTER AND WATER SEPARATOR

Turbocharger

A *turbocharger* boosts engine power by increasing the volume of air/fuel mixture delivered to an engine. A turbocharger uses an *air compressor* to increase air pressure in an intake manifold and this additional pressure forces extra air/fuel mixture into the combustion chambers. This extra fuel increases engine power.

A turbocharger is often used to increase power in small engines. Some designs use full-time turbochargers that continuously regulate pressure in the manifold, while others only engage when an accelerator pedal is pushed to the floor and extra power is needed.

A turbocharger directs engine exhaust fumes against the blades of a *turbine*. These powerful exhaust gases can rotate a turbine up to 140,000 revolutions per minute (a crankshaft typically turns 3,000 rpm). This strong rotating force operates the air compressor that packs extra air/fuel mixture into the combustion chambers.

A *supercharger* is another device used to increase air pressure in an intake manifold. A supercharger, however, uses a belt drive from the engine, rather than exhaust gases, to power the air compressor.

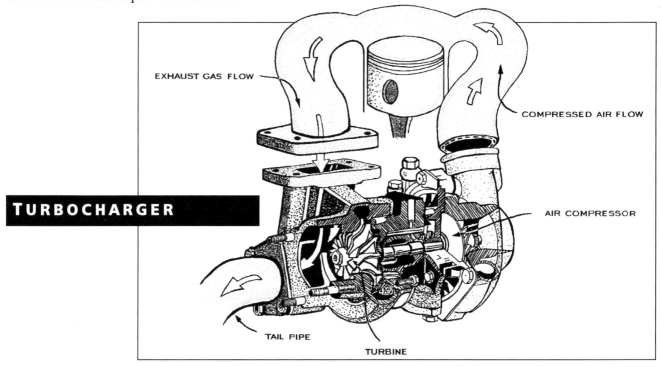

EXHAUST GAS FLOW

COMPRESSED AIR FLOW

TURBOCHARGER

AIR COMPRESSOR

TAIL PIPE

TURBINE

Emission Controls

*P*ositive crankcase ventilation (PCV) was the first emissions control device. The PCV system uses a simple rubber hose to carry polluting fumes from an engine's crankcase to an air cleaner, carburetor body, or intake manifold. These fumes are then added to the air/fuel mixture and burned a second time. This reburning further destroys hydrocarbon vapor, and other harmful emissions. A one-way, *PCV valve* prevents explosive fumes from going the wrong way and entering a crankcase.

The *exhaust gas recirculation* (EGR) system represents a second generation pollution control mechanism. This arrangement pumps exhaust fumes into an intake manifold. As with the PCV system, harmful fumes are mixed with the air/fuel mixture for reburning.

A third type of pollution control system is the *air injection* method. With this system, fresh air is pumped into an *exhaust manifold* to mix with exhaust fumes as they leave an engine. The fresh air increases oxidation, further destroying harmful hydrocarbons.

The *catalytic converter* is another mechanism used to decrease pollutants. A catalytic converter is usually located under a car and looks like a large, flat muffler. This device contains compounds that react with hydrocarbons in exhaust gases and chemically converts them to water and other less harmful compounds. Some vehicles have two catalytic converters, one under the car and a smaller one attached to the exhaust manifold.

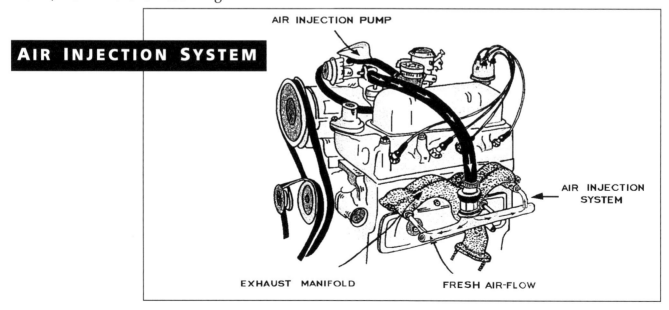

AIR INJECTION SYSTEM

AIR INJECTION PUMP

AIR INJECTION SYSTEM

EXHAUST MANIFOLD

FRESH AIR-FLOW

Exhaust Manifold & Muffler

An *exhaust manifold* collects exhaust gases from the combustion chambers and funnels them into the relativity small area of an *exhaust pipe*. A "V" shaped engine must have two exhaust manifolds, one on each side of the "V."

A *muffler* reduces engine noise by using a series of passageways, *baffles*, and compartments to trap sound. An exhaust pipe carries exhaust fumes away from the passenger compartment, to the muffler, and out the *tail pipe*.

EXHAUST SYSTEM

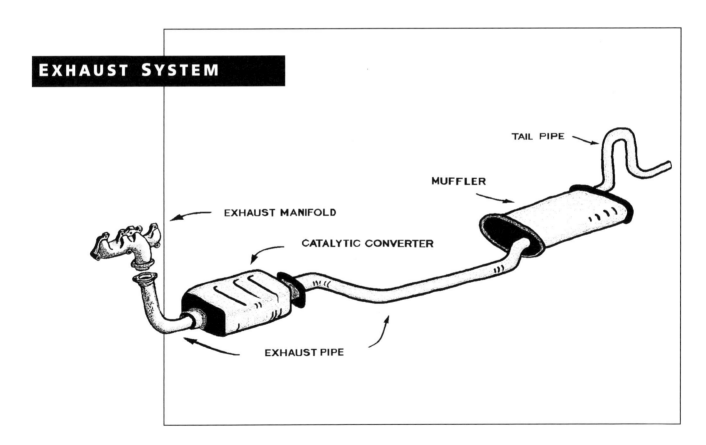

TAIL PIPE

MUFFLER

EXHAUST MANIFOLD

CATALYTIC CONVERTER

EXHAUST PIPE

FUEL SYSTEM TEST

Identify the parts:

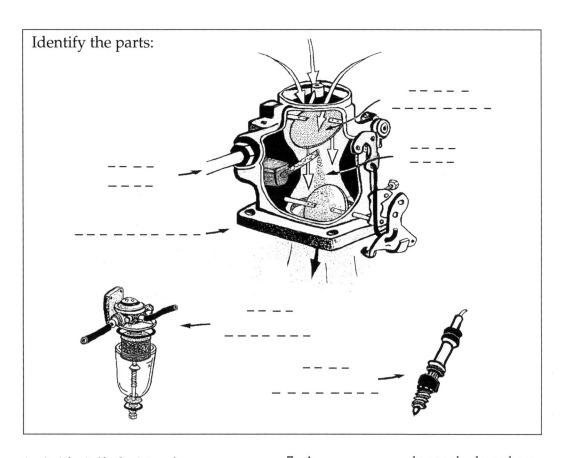

1. A rich air/fuel mixture has more _____ and less_____. *(p. 32)*

2. The two types of air/fuel mixers are _____ & _____. *(p. 31)*

3. A supercharger increases air pressure in an exhaust manifold. (T) or(F) *(p. 38)*

4. A BARO sensor measures _____pressure. *(p. 34)*

5. A butterfly valve controls fuel _____. *(p. 32)*

6. _____fuel injection uses a single injector in a carburetor body. *(p. 33)*

7. A _____ changes hydrocarbons to less harmful compounds. *(p. 39)*

8. Gasoline tank_____ are used to stop fuel from sloshing. *(p. 35)*

9. A _____ _____is used to trap gasoline fumes. *(p. 35)*

10. Only mechanical fuel pumps are used in gasoline tanks. (T) or (F) *(p. 36)*

11. A turbocharger uses _____to rotate a turbine. *(p. 38)*

12. An air/fuel mixture enters combustion chambers through the_____ valve openings. *(p. 17)*

CHAPTER FOUR

Cooling System

A *cooling system* uses a mixture of water and *antifreeze* to absorb and disperse engine heat. This mixture, called *coolant*, is pushed through a cooling system by a *water pump*. The coolant flows around the outside of the combustion chambers and absorbs heat. The hot coolant then circulates to a *radiator* where excess heat radiates to the outside air.

A cooling system has three jobs:

1. Dispersing excess engine heat
2. Quickly heating a cold engine
3. Maintaining the proper engine running temperature

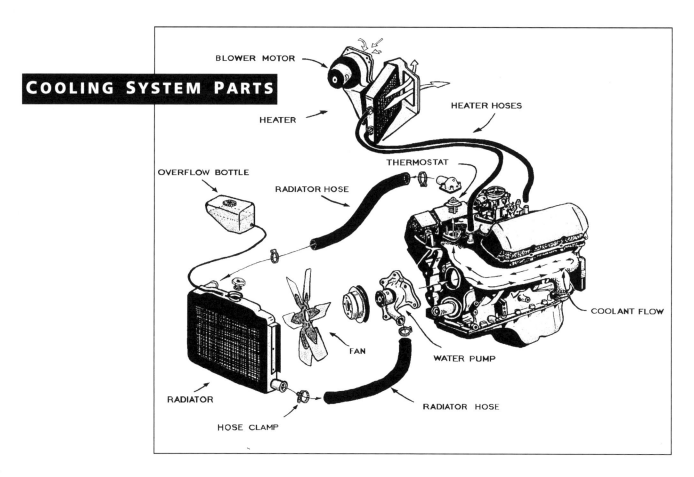

COOLING SYSTEM PARTS

BLOWER MOTOR

HEATER

HEATER HOSES

OVERFLOW BOTTLE

RADIATOR HOSE

THERMOSTAT

COOLANT FLOW

FAN

WATER PUMP

RADIATOR

HOSE CLAMP

RADIATOR HOSE

Radiator

A *radiator* efficiently transfers heat from liquid coolant to the surrounding air. Hot coolant enters at the top of a radiator and flows down to the bottom through small copper pipes. Fins attached to the pipes increase the surface area exposed to the air. As air passes over the fins, heat is conducted to the moving air-flow and carried away. By the time coolant gets to the bottom of a radiator, it has cooled enough to absorb another dose of heat.

An engine operates more efficiently at temperatures above the boiling point of water. As an engine heats, coolant expands inside the system, increasing pressure. The greater pressure raises the boiling point of the coolant, allowing an engine to run at the higher temperatures without boiling the coolant. If pressure becomes too great, a spring-loaded pressure release *radiator cap* automatically opens so coolant can escape the system, thus relieving the pressure. This overflow coolant is saved in a *reservoir bottle* or *overflow bottle* located to the side of an engine compartment. As an engine cools, coolant volume in a radiator shrinks, drawing back the overflow coolant. This is how coolant added to a plastic reservoir bottle is returned to a radiator.

Separate radiators may be used to cool transmission fluid, engine oil, freon gas, and turbochargers (*intercooler* radiators). A separate radiator also delivers heat to a passenger compartment and defrosters.

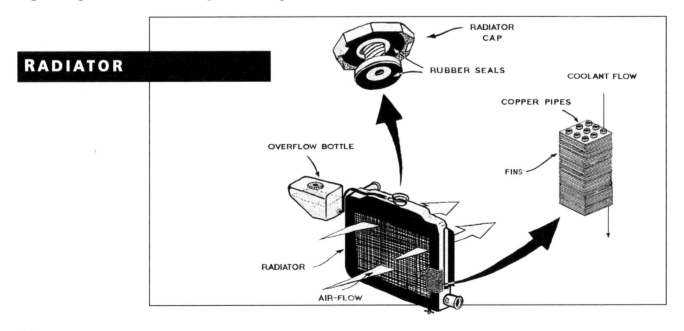

RADIATOR

RADIATOR CAP

RUBBER SEALS

COOLANT FLOW

COPPER PIPES

OVERFLOW BOTTLE

FINS

RADIATOR

AIR-FLOW

Thermostat

A *thermostat* maintains a steady engine temperature by regulating the amount of coolant flowing through a system. If an engine is cold, a thermostat blocks coolant flow, allowing an engine to heat-up quickly. As an engine warms, a thermostat automatically opens to allow the coolant to circulate. When proper engine temperature is reached, a thermostat maintains that temperature by slightly opening or closing to compensate for engine load, vehicle speed, and outside air temperature. A balance is thus maintained between coolant flow and proper engine temperature.

A thermostat is usually located on the top of an engine, often inside a rounded metal cover cap. A *thermostat cap* is usually at the end of the large rubber hose leading from the top of a radiator to an engine. This radiator hose almost always attaches directly to the metal cap that houses a thermostat.

Modern thermostats use a metal pellet containing a special wax that rapidly expands and contracts with changing coolant temperature. When temperature increases, the wax expands inside the pellet and pushes out a rod and *thermostat valve*, opening the thermostat and increasing the coolant flow.

Although part of a cooling system, a thermostat actually heats an engine by closing off the coolant flow. Without this warm-up feature an engine might never reach its proper operating temperature, especially on cold days, thus disabling the heater and defroster when needed most.

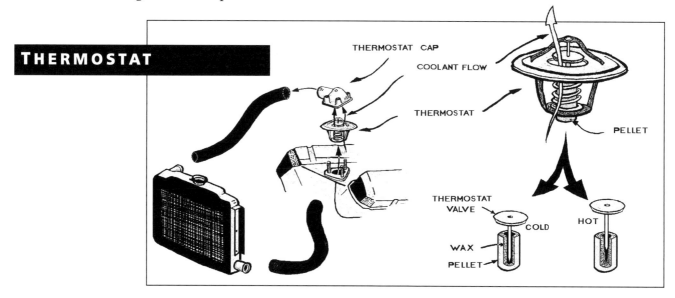

THERMOSTAT

THERMOSTAT CAP

COOLANT FLOW

THERMOSTAT

PELLET

THERMOSTAT VALVE

COLD

HOT

WAX

PELLET

Water Pump

A *water pump* circulates coolant through a cooling system with an internal paddle wheel or *impeller*. The impeller is turned by a *fan belt*, or *drive belt*, connected to the crankshaft pulley. The faster a crankshaft turns, the faster coolant circulates.

Water pumps are at the front of an engine where they can conveniently use a drive belt from a crankshaft pulley. The same drive belt, sometimes called a *serpentine belt,* often spins other accessories, such as an alternator, power steering pump, smog control pump, air conditioning compressor, or cooling fan.

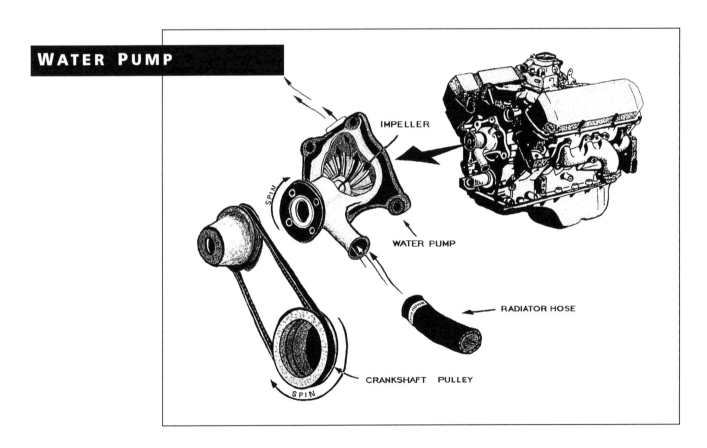

WATER PUMP

IMPELLER

WATER PUMP

RADIATOR HOSE

CRANKSHAFT PULLEY

SPIN

SPIN

Cooling Fan

A *cooling fan* creates an air flow when a car is stopped or moving slowly. Air must flow over the fins in a radiator to carry away enough heat to cool an engine. Fans rotate either by a fan belt from a crankshaft or a small electric motor.

A *thermal fan* engages only when coolant temperature is too high; most of the time a thermal fan is disengaged and not moving. This saves energy and reduces engine noise.

With a forward-facing engine, a cooling fan attaches to a water pump at the front of an engine, directly behind the radiator. With an engine facing forward, a fan and water pump are easily powered by the drive belt from the crankcase pulley.

With a transverse-mounted engine, the engine, crankshaft pulley, and drive belts all face sideways. A fan mounted to the front of this engine arrangement would face sideways and not help the air-flow. So a cooling fan, still mounted behind a radiator, is used, powered by a remote electric motor, switched on and off by signals from a temperature sensor.

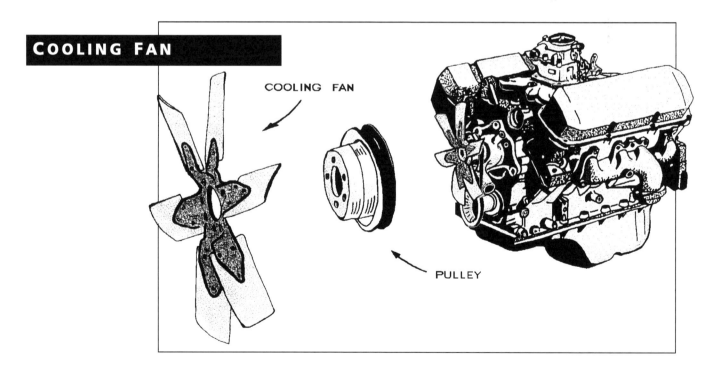

COOLING FAN

COOLING FAN

PULLEY

Hoses

Two radiator *hoses* carry coolant between a radiator and an engine. These thick rubber hoses have layers of fabric reinforcement molded into them. Some have metal springs inside to prevent kinking and collapsing. An upper radiator hose connects to the top of a radiator and delivers hot coolant from an engine to a radiator. A lower radiator hose, connects to the bottom of a radiator and delivers coolant to a water pump. Smaller hoses, the *heater hoses*, carry coolant to a separate *heater* radiator in the pas-senger compartment.

Coolant must continuously circulate to prevent the creation of hot water pockets inside an engine block. For this reason a small *by-pass hose* creates a trickle flow of coolant through an engine, even when a thermostat has "closed" the coolant flow.

Many other hoses are used in cars, including fuel lines, oil cooler, transmission fluid, vacuum, emissions, freon, and brake fluid hoses. A variety of *hose clamps* are used to secure these hoses.

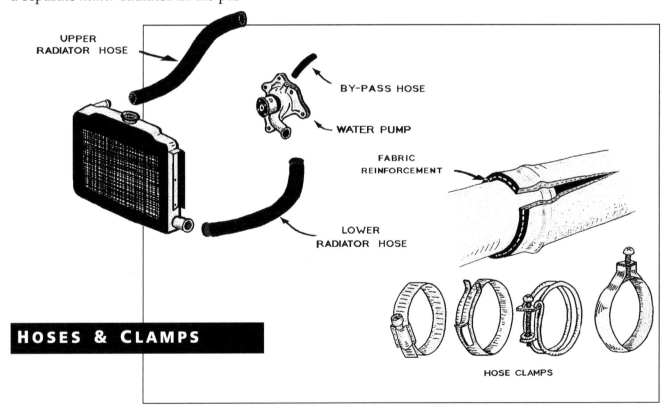

UPPER RADIATOR HOSE

BY-PASS HOSE

WATER PUMP

FABRIC REINFORCEMENT

LOWER RADIATOR HOSE

HOSE CLAMPS

HOSES & CLAMPS

Heater & Defroster

A car heater uses excess heat from a cooling system to warm a passenger compartment. Heater hoses carry hot coolant to and from a small radiator under the dashboard. An electric fan, or *blower*, blows air over the hot radiator fins, carrying warm air through ducts and vents and into a passenger compartment. The amount of heat is governed by the speed of the fan and the amount of coolant flow. A heating system and *air conditioning* system usually share the same duct and vent system and the same blower fan and motor.

The hot air from a heater can also be directed to the inside of a windshield to *defrost* a windshield. A small electric heating wire is often built into the glass of a rear window to act as an electric defroster.

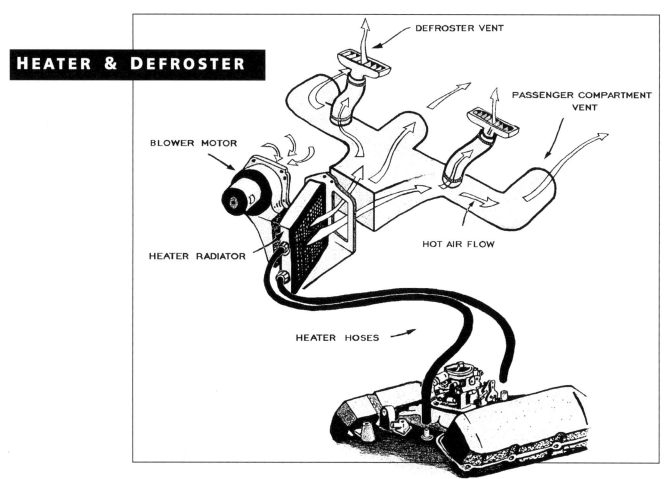

HEATER & DEFROSTER

DEFROSTER VENT

PASSENGER COMPARTMENT VENT

BLOWER MOTOR

HEATER RADIATOR

HOT AIR FLOW

HEATER HOSES

COOLING SYSTEM TEST

Identify the parts:

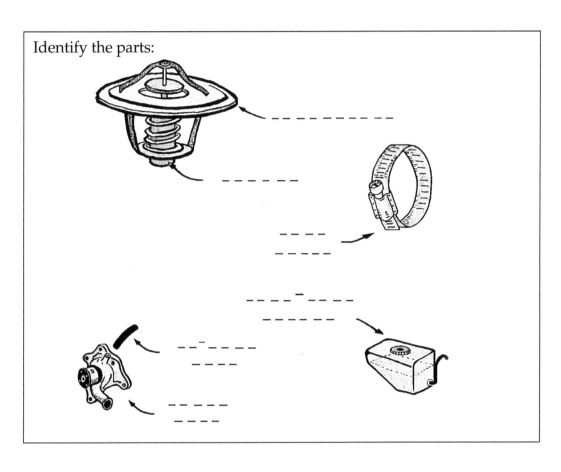

1. A thermostat helps to heat a cold engine. (T) (F) *(p. 45)*

2. A cooling fan supplements the _____ through a radiator. *(p. 47)*

3. An internal "paddle wheel" inside a pump is called an _____. *(p. 46)*

4. As an engine warms, coolant_____, increasing pressure in the system. *(p. 44)*

5. Water is mixed with _____ to make coolant. *(p. 43)*

6. Only_____hoses carry coolant to and from a radiator. *(p. 48)*

7. Increased pressure raises the boiling point of coolant. (T) (F) *(p. 44)*

8. A _____ hose creates a trickle flow of coolant through the system. *(p. 48)*

9. A car heater takes heat from the cooling system. (T) (F). *(p. 49)*

10. If a car heater only blows cool air. What does this suggest? *(p. 45)* _____
_____

11. A car overheats but there is plenty of coolant. What does this suggest?_____
_____

CHAPTER FIVE

Running Gear

The *running gear* includes the parts used to guide a vehicle through bumps, swerves, and road hazards. The running gear connects a driver to the roadway and helps negotiate rough roads, sharp turns, and fast stops, all while keeping a constant weight on all four tires. If bouncing and bumps cause one tire to even slightly leave a roadway, this will adversely affect a vehicle's steering, cornering, and braking, especially dangerous in extreme conditions, when control is needed the most.

Parts from the *suspension*, *steering*, and *wheels* keep tires on the road and a driver in control.

RUNNING GEAR

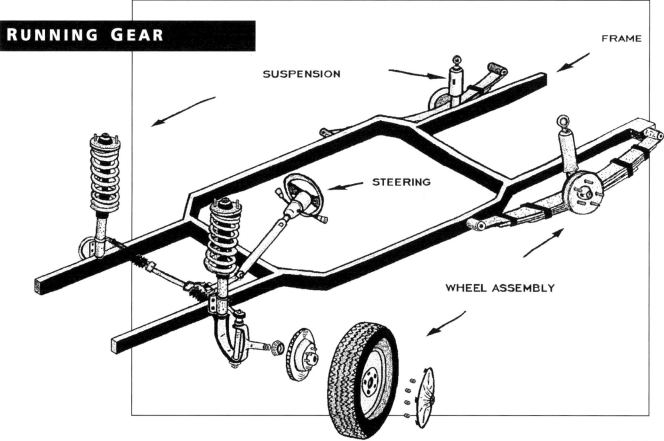

FRAME

SUSPENSION

STEERING

WHEEL ASSEMBLY

Frame

A *frame* is a solid base for all car parts: engine, tires, doors, windows, seats, and the driver and passengers.

Two basic frame designs are used:
1. Platform
2. Unibody

A *platform* system is a solid series of steel beams welded together to form a large base or platform supporting all other car parts. Specific platform design varies for each car model.

A *unibody* system uses *fenders*, *floorboards*, *firewall*, and other body parts, rather than a separate platform, to provide rigid structure. The body parts themselves, welded together, provide the necessary strength to support the weight of a vehicle, eliminating the heavy platform. Modern *crumple-zone* body construction adds greater collision protection.

A frame must be as insulated as possible from road bumps to control the momentum of the heavy load it carries. This control, provided by the *suspension*, keeps the tires in even contact with the road and gives passengers a smooth ride.

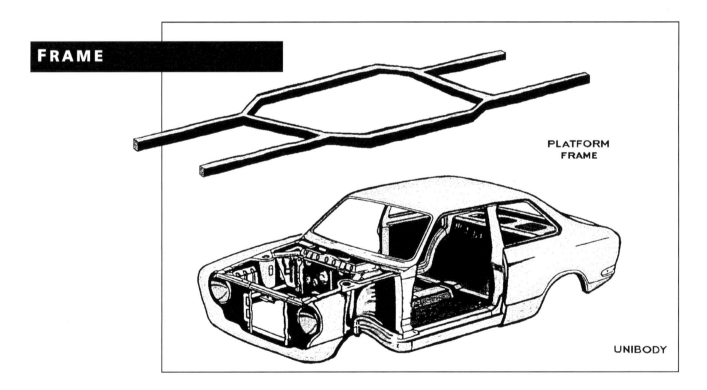

FRAME

PLATFORM FRAME

UNIBODY

Suspension

A *suspension* system provides the connection between a frame and the *wheel assemblies.* This connection must absorb bumps and twists, while keeping an equal distribution of weight on each tire. Modern systems use separate, *independent suspension,* for all four wheels. Two common types are shown below; there are many variations.

A suspension system is responsible for:
1. Maintaining the same weight on each tire at all times
2. Keeping a car level
3. Insulating passengers from road bumps and sways

A *stabilizer bar*, or *sway bar*, transfers lifting force to the opposite wheel to help level a vehicle when cornering. *Leaf springs, coil springs, torsion bars, struts,* and *shock absorbers* are just a few of the many types of suspension parts. High-tech systems such as the Electronic Stability Program (ESP) use computers to monitor and control suspension parts.

Vehicles which carry heavy loads or go off-road are equipped with stronger, stiffer suspensions which absorb more extreme motion but give passengers a rougher ride.

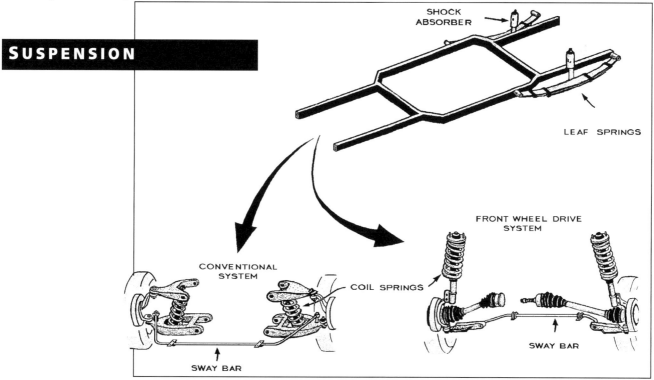

SUSPENSION

SHOCK ABSORBER

LEAF SPRINGS

CONVENTIONAL SYSTEM

COIL SPRINGS

FRONT WHEEL DRIVE SYSTEM

SWAY BAR

SWAY BAR

Springs

Suspension *springs* provide a steel cushion between the wheels and a frame. This cushion absorbs bumps, insulates passengers, and helps equalize weight on all four wheels.

Three types of springs are used in suspension systems:
1. Leaf springs
2. Coil springs
3. Torsion bars

Leaf springs are made from several long strips of steel, bolted together. The iron strips spring back to their original position after a bounce. Sliding and scraping between the strips can be noisy and create a harsh ride, so a single fiberglass leaf may be used. Leaf springs are almost always used on the rear wheels.

Coil springs support the front ends of most cars. Like leaf springs, these thick metal coils return to their original position after distortion. Coil springs are often located between the upper and lower *control arms*. Two pivoting control arms are called a *double wishbone* system.

Torsion bars look like plain steel rods but act like coil springs because of a built-in twist. Torsion bars are space saving devices. The degree of spring is built into torsion bars during the forging process.

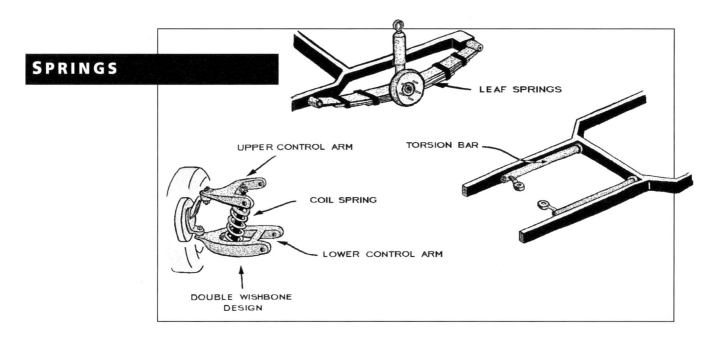

SPRINGS

LEAF SPRINGS

UPPER CONTROL ARM

TORSION BAR

COIL SPRING

LOWER CONTROL ARM

DOUBLE WISHBONE DESIGN

Shock Absorbers

A *shock absorber* stabilizes or dampens the up and down bouncing of the springs. Shock absorbers work only when a car bounces. At rest they have no function.

A shock absorber is a sealed cylinder filled with hydraulic fluid with a plunger/piston inside. When a car bounces, the shock absorber piston is forced through the fluid. The resistant force of the fluid on the piston dampens the bouncing. Small valves inside regulate the flow of fluid, determining the absorption characteristics of each shock absorber. Pressurized gas is also used in some shock absorbers in combination with hydraulic fluid.

A *MacPherson strut* is a special kind of shock absorber that incorporates a coil spring and a shock absorber in a single unit. MacPherson struts are often used in front wheel drive vehicles to save space. A variety of other struts and shocks can be used, including: *Iso struts, Chapman struts,* and a wide selection of special *shocks*.

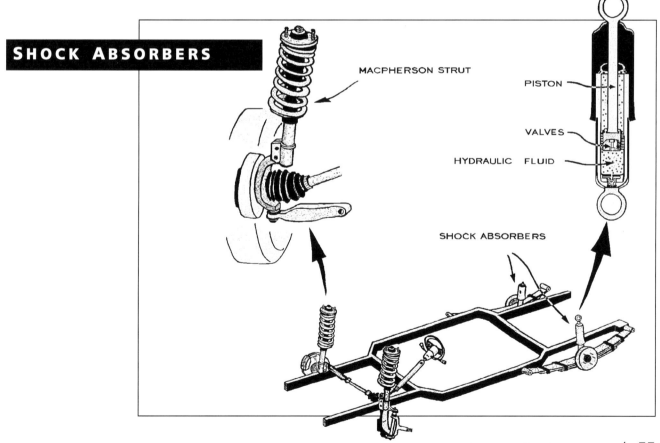

SHOCK ABSORBERS

MACPHERSON STRUT

PISTON

VALVES

HYDRAULIC FLUID

SHOCK ABSORBERS

Steering

A *steering column* and the *steering gear* are the two basic parts of a steering system. A steering wheel column contains not only the means to control a car's direction but may contain many complex electrical connections between driver and car, including the ignition key switch, horn, headlight controls, cruise control, turn signal controls, windshield wipers, and washers.

There are two fundamental types of steering gear systems: *worm gear* and *rack and pinion*. With a *worm gear steering* system, also called the *recirculating ball system*, a steering wheel column extends to a *steering box* which transfers motion from a steering wheel to the front wheels. To reduce friction, ball bearings are placed in the grooves of the *worm gear* and travel along the grooves as it rotates. A steering box also increases the turning power or *mechanical advantage* of a steering wheel, through the pitman arm.

A *rack and pinion* steering system uses a sliding flat gear called a rack and a round stationary *pinion* gear fixed to the end of a steering column. As it rotates, the pinion gear moves the rack back and forth. The front wheel assemblies attach to each end of the rack with universal joints. Rubber boots protect the gears and joints from dirt and moisture and hold in lubricating fluid. This system provides smooth, steady, but somewhat stiffer steering.

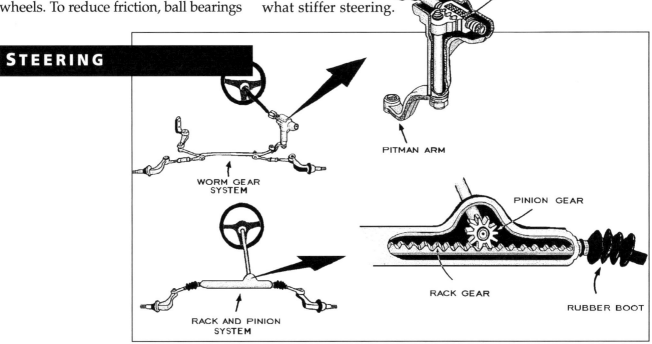

STEERING

BALL BEARINGS

PITMAN ARM

WORM GEAR SYSTEM

RACK AND PINION SYSTEM

PINION GEAR

RACK GEAR

RUBBER BOOT

Power Steering

Power steering provides extra steering power, which is especially helpful with large vehicles and when parking. Both hydraulic and electric systems are used.

Hydraulic power steering uses fluid pressure to assist front wheel turning. Turning a steering wheel activates valves which direct pressurized fluid against surfaces inside a *steering box*. This additional pressure adds to the force from a driver's hand on a steering wheel. A power steering unit may be used with either worm drive or rack and pinion mechanisms but is more common with worm drive units. A *power steering pump* supplies the force behind the hydraulic fluid. A *fluid reservoir,* which attaches to the top of a power steering pump, is the place to check the hydraulic fluid level and to add more if necessary.

Electric power steering uses an electric motor that activates only when a steering wheel is moved. This motorized system is considerably simpler than the hydraulic method and represents a new generation of power steering systems.

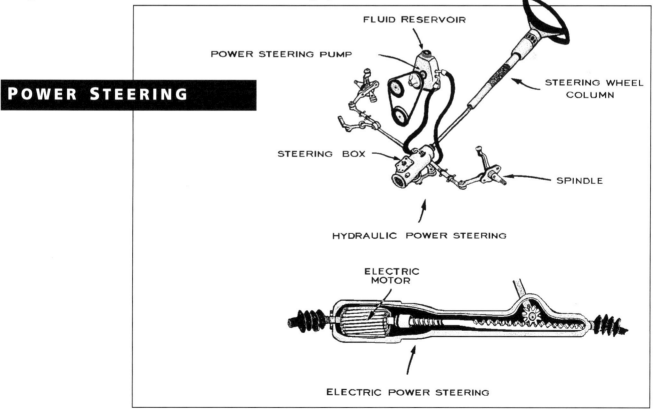

POWER STEERING

FLUID RESERVOIR

POWER STEERING PUMP

STEERING WHEEL COLUMN

STEERING BOX

SPINDLE

HYDRAULIC POWER STEERING

ELECTRIC MOTOR

ELECTRIC POWER STEERING

Ball Joints

Ball joints make a strong moveable or hinged connection between moving parts in the suspension and steering systems. Ball joints are used in the upper and lower control arms, the steering bars or *tie rods*, and a variety of other locations.

Tie rods connect the steering gear and the two wheels; a *tie rod end* threads onto a tie rod and thus provides a mechanism for adjusting front-end alignment. A tie rod end contains the ball joint and is replaced as a unit when a new ball joint is needed. Ball joints are often equipped with *wear indicators* for easy inspection and *zerk* fittings for injecting lubricating grease.

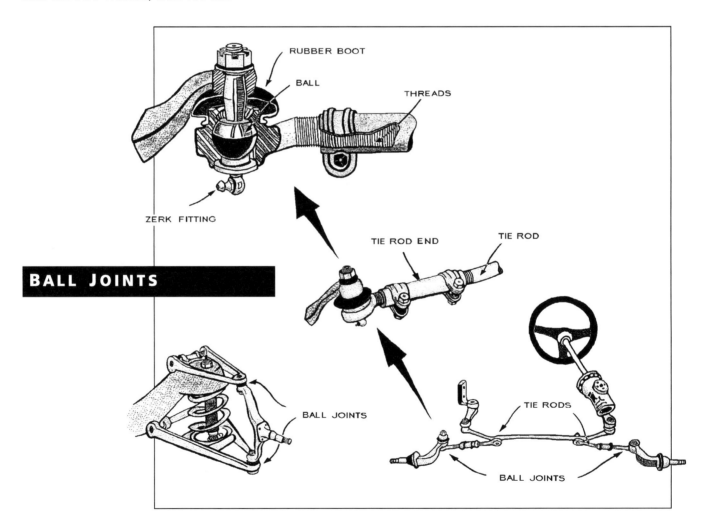

BALL JOINTS

RUBBER BOOT
BALL
THREADS
ZERK FITTING
TIE ROD END
TIE ROD
BALL JOINTS
TIE RODS
BALL JOINTS

Wheels

A car *wheel* is a combination of a rubber *tire* and metal *rim*. Wheels bolt to a *brake drum, rotor, axle,* or *spindle* with *lug* nuts, often located behind the *hubcap*.

A *steering knuckle* and *spindle* pass through a wheel assembly and extend into a *wheel hub*. *Wheel bearings* inside a hub surround and attach the wheel to a spindle shaft or brake drum. The many roller bearings contained in a wheel bearing provide the only contact points between a moving wheel and the stationary spindle.

Rear wheel drive vehicles, trucks, and trailers often use solid axle systems that directly connect the two rear wheels. This connection is less desirable because bumps that might be absorbed by a single wheel are now transferred to the opposite wheel. With *independent suspension* on all four wheels the transfer of this motion is eliminated, providing a smoother ride.

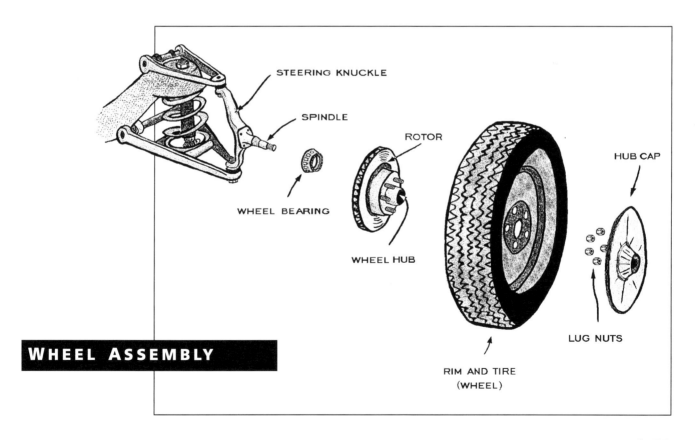

STEERING KNUCKLE

SPINDLE

ROTOR

HUB CAP

WHEEL BEARING

WHEEL HUB

LUG NUTS

RIM AND TIRE
(WHEEL)

WHEEL ASSEMBLY

Tires

Almost all cars use *radial* tires. The *plies*, or layers, in radial tires are arranged to reduce movement between the plies. This radial construction prevents overheating, reduces wear, and improves gas mileage. Other tire types such as bias ply, belted bias ply, and recaps are used mostly by trucks and commercial vehicles.

A *tread pattern* is the footprint of a tire. A driver influences the speed or direction of a car only where rubber touches the road. Without tread, a tire cannot direct water and gravel aside.

Many special tread patterns exist:

1. Snow tires—designed with large grooves to dig in and give extra traction

2. Mud and snow tires—a compromise between regular tires and snow tires
3. Rain tires—designed to push out water from under a tire
4. Slicks—drag racing tires made completely smooth; the smoothness helps disperse heat

The weight of a car and tire pressure determine the amount of rubber that touches a road. Regardless of tire width or tread design, the total area of rubber touching a road is exactly the same for a given car weight and tire pressure. Bald tires are dangerous because the tread pattern has worn away, not because there is less surface area touching the road.

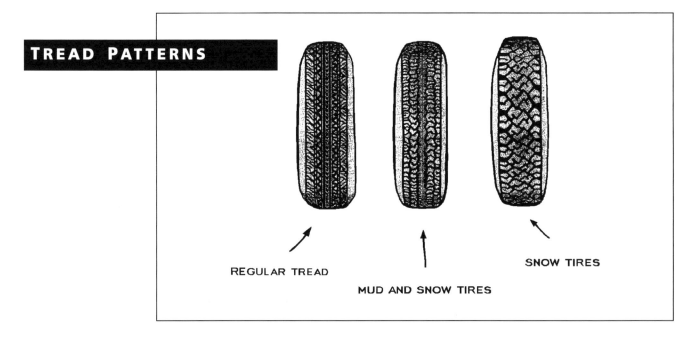

TREAD PATTERNS

REGULAR TREAD

MUD AND SNOW TIRES

SNOW TIRES

RUNNING GEAR TEST

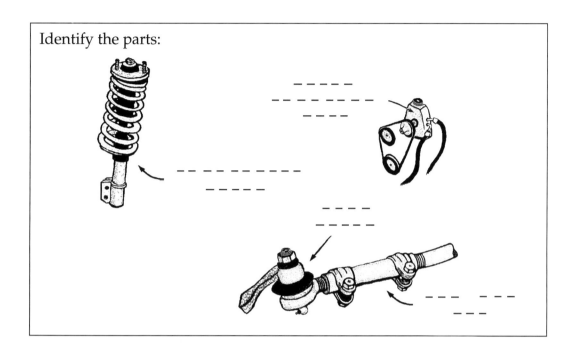

Identify the parts:

1. A_____contains a ball joint. *(p. 58)*

2. Almost all car tires are_____ ply. *(p. 60)*

3. A_____ _____ is a combination shock absorber and coil spring. *(p. 55)*

4. A_____ frame uses fenders and other body parts to support a car. *(p. 52)*

5. Sway bars help level a car when cornering. (T) (F) *(p. 53)*

6. Leaf springs are usually used on the (front) (rear) of a vehicle. *(p. 54)*

7. Torsion bars are twisted _____ of steel. *(p. 54)*

8. A_____ dampens the bouncing of the springs. *(p.55)*

9. A shock absorber uses _____ _____ to slow the plunger. *(p. 55)*

10. A worm gear steering system uses a pinion gear. (T) (F) *(p. 56)*

11. A _____ is lubricated through a _____ fitting. *(p. 58)*

12. Shock absorbers only work when a car is moving. (T) (F) *(p. 55)*

13. Wheel bearings are located in a _____. *(p. 59)*

14. Running gear keep a driver in control and the _____on the road. *(p. 51)*

15. If a car continues to bounce following a bump, replace the_____. *(p. 55)*

CHAPTER SIX

Brakes

A *braking system* controls how fast, how smooth, and how straight a car slows down. Automobile braking systems use *master cylinders* and *hydraulic fluid* to transfer force from a *brake pedal* to *friction pads* located inside each wheel assembly. These friction pads are forced against metal surfaces in each wheel to create the friction which slows a car; the harder a pedal is pressed, the more friction is applied.

Force from a foot pedal must be equally balanced between all four wheels, delivering the same force at exactly the same time to each wheel.

Otherwise, one wheel would slow down sooner than the others, causing a vehicle to swerve or "pull" to the side—or worse, locking a wheel and causing a skid.

There are two types of braking systems:
1. *Disc brakes*, where pads held in *calipers* pinch against the spinning *rotors*
2. *Drum brakes*, where *wheel cylinders* push pads against *brake drums*

Vehicles often use a combination, with discs on the front and drums on the rear. Many modern vehicles employ disc brakes on all four wheels.

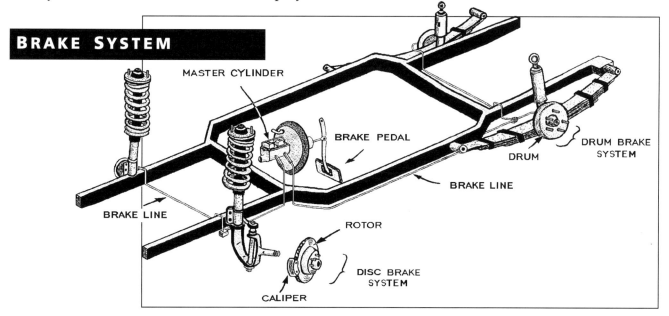

BRAKE SYSTEM

MASTER CYLINDER

BRAKE PEDAL

DRUM BRAKE SYSTEM

DRUM

BRAKE LINE

BRAKE LINE

ROTOR

DISC BRAKE SYSTEM

CALIPER

Master Cylinder

A *brake pedal* is a pump handle for a *master cylinder*. Almost all master cylinders are divided into two separate systems. If one fails, the other one will keep at least two brakes working, providing some braking despite the partial hydraulic failure.

Sensitive *pressure regulators* ensure that all friction pads receive the same braking power at exactly the same time. Pressure regulators are located between a master cylinder and the wheels. A *metering valve* coordinates the time when disc and drum brakes engage the wheels. A *proportional valve* balances the pressure between the front and rear brakes. Modern auto makers may use a *combination valve*, which does both jobs.

Larger vehicles use *power brakes* to increase the force from a foot pedal. Two types are used: a vacuum *booster* system (shown below) which uses vacuum from the intake manifold to increase the pedal force, and an *electro-hydraulic* system which uses an electric motor to increase hydraulic force. Pedal force can also be amplified using a system which shares fluid from the nearby power steering system.

A master cylinder provides a reservoir where fluid level is checked and new fluid is added. Most master cylinders have a sensor in the reservoir to signal low fluid and a pressure sensitive switch to turn on the brake lights.

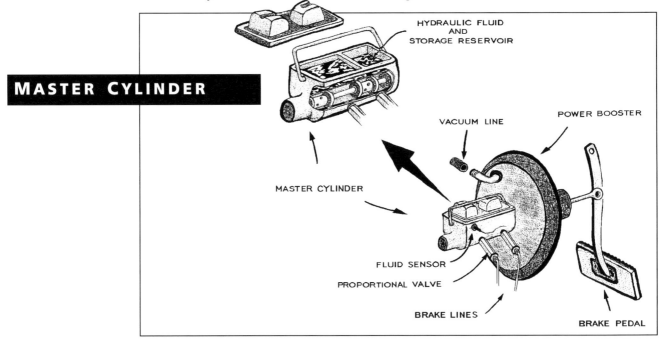

MASTER CYLINDER

HYDRAULIC FLUID
AND
STORAGE RESERVOIR

VACUUM LINE

POWER BOOSTER

MASTER CYLINDER

FLUID SENSOR

PROPORTIONAL VALVE

BRAKE LINES

BRAKE PEDAL

Disc Brakes

A *disc brake* system uses a polished metal disc or *rotor* and *friction pads,* which pinch against the rotor, to slow a car. Typically, each wheel assembly in the disc brake system has a rotor, a *caliper,* and two friction pads, one positioned on each side of the rotor. A *caliper* positions the friction pads and transfers hydraulic force from a master cylinder to the friction pads. A rotor and pads are often partially visible through the wheel *spokes.* Both a tire and a rim bolt to a rotor and all rotate together when a car is moving.

Small metal pipes called *brake lines* carry the hydraulic fluid from a master cylinder to the calipers at each wheel. Friction pads are held inside calipers about one hundredth (.01) of an inch from the rotor. Alignment and timing between all rotors, friction pads and calipers must be precise to avoid vibrations and squeaking when the pads touch the rotors.

Friction from braking creates considerable heat, but the open-air design of the disc system allows rapid heat dispersion.

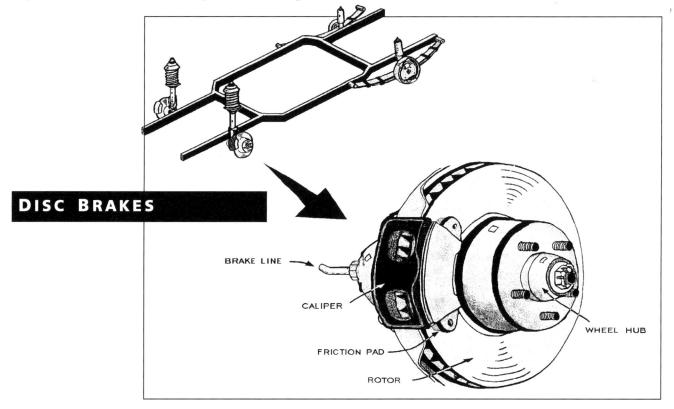

DISC BRAKES

BRAKE LINE →

CALIPER

FRICTION PAD

ROTOR

WHEEL HUB

Drum Brakes

In the *drum brake* system, curved friction pads, called *brake shoes*, are pushed out against a *brake drum* when hydraulic fluid from a master cylinder is received at each of the *wheel cylinders*. One wheel cylinder, one brake drum and two brake shoes are located at each drum brake wheel assembly.

A *brake drum* is like a bowl with smooth surfaces on the inner sides. Brake shoes are pushed outward against these surfaces when a brake pedal is pushed. When a pedal is released, strong springs pull the shoes away from the drum, forcing fluid back through the brake lines and into the master cylinder reservoir (see p. 64).

A *wheel cylinder*, located between each pair of shoes, receives and transforms hydraulic fluid from the master cylinder into the mechanical pushing force used to press brake shoes against a drum. Like a disc brake rotor, a brake drum attaches to a vehicle at a wheel hub, spindle, or axle using wheel bearings to reduce friction. Also, like the disc brake rotor, a tire and rim bolt directly to the outside of the wheel drum (see p. 59).

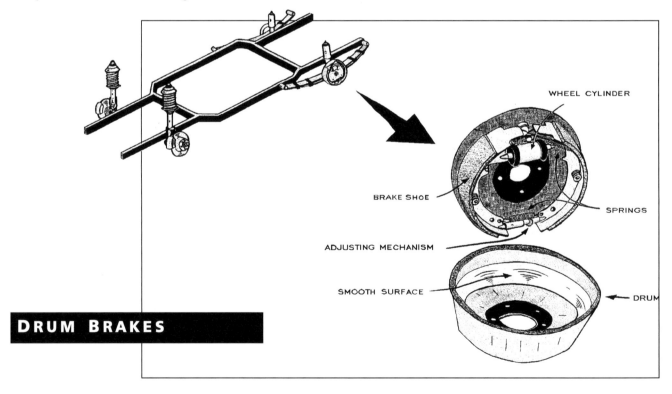

DRUM BRAKES

WHEEL CYLINDER

BRAKE SHOE

SPRINGS

ADJUSTING MECHANISM

SMOOTH SURFACE

DRUM

Friction Pads

Friction pads must withstand extreme pressures and temperatures, yet be soft enough to protect the smooth polished surfaces of a wheel drum or rotor. Friction pads must also maintain a similar degree of friction, *the coefficient of friction,* throughout a wide range of temperature and weather conditions. This insures even braking.

Friction pads used in drum brakes are called *brake shoes.* New friction pad material, or brake *linings,* attach to metal *backing plates.* Friction pads in disc brake systems are usually called pads or *disc pads.*

In either system if the pad material wears down completely, the metal backing plate will touch the wheel drum or rotor and scratch, or *score,* the smooth surfaces. In some vehicles a signal warns that friction pads are wearing thin.

Tremendous heat is generated in the braking process. A stop from 60 mph can heat the brake shoes to 450° F. Disc pads, which require 10 times the force, can heat to 1000° F. Like the heat generated in an engine, the heat from braking dissipates to the surrounding air.

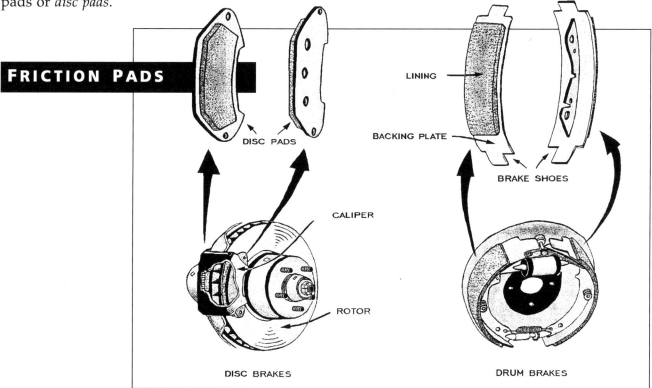

FRICTION PADS

DISC PADS

CALIPER

ROTOR

DISC BRAKES

LINING

BACKING PLATE

BRAKE SHOES

DRUM BRAKES

Anti-lock Brake System

The computerized *anti-lock brake system* (ABS) virtually eliminates uncontrolled tire skids. Slamming on regular brakes at highway speed will "lock-up" or completely stop a tire, causing it to skid. The long swerving skid marks on the highway are the result of brakes stopping tires, but not stopping the car. The ABS system prevents this type of skidding.

With ABS, a computer counts each time a wheel makes a revolution. Under normal driving conditions all four wheels turn the same speed. If one wheel locks-up during braking, the wheel count for that wheel will immediately drop to zero. This triggers the release of the brake mechanism for that wheel, allowing it to rotate freely. When the rotation count becomes equal again, the computer will reactivate the braking mechanism for that wheel. During hard braking, this process results in rapid "on-and-off" skidding for each wheel, leaving dotted skid marks down a roadway.

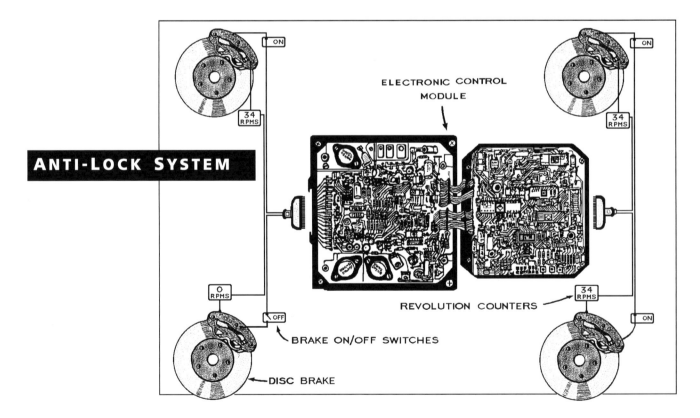

ANTI-LOCK SYSTEM

ELECTRONIC CONTROL MODULE

34 RPMS · ON · 34 RPMS · ON · 0 RPMS · OFF · 34 RPMS · ON

REVOLUTION COUNTERS

BRAKE ON/OFF SWITCHES

DISC BRAKE

Parking Brake

A *parking brake* stops a car from rolling away when parked. Parking brakes operate either by hand or foot using levers and cables to connect to the wheels; this mechanical linkage is independent of the hydraulic system.

A parking brake system is usually limited to only two wheels. The rear wheels are usually used for the parking brake with rear wheel drive vehicles. Front wheel drive vehicles often use the front two wheels for the parking brake. Parking brake systems usually share the friction pads, drums, or rotors of the regular braking system. Vehicles with disc brakes on all four wheels sometimes use an independent parking brake system, connecting to an axle instead of a wheel.

A parking brake may be used as an *emergency brake* to slow a vehicle if complete brake failure occurs.

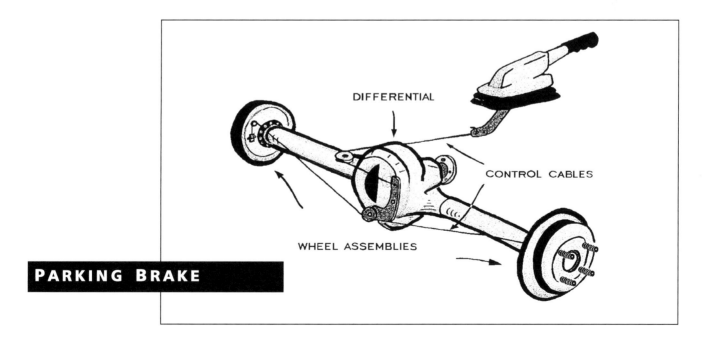

DIFFERENTIAL

CONTROL CABLES

WHEEL ASSEMBLIES

PARKING BRAKE

BRAKE TEST

Identify the parts:

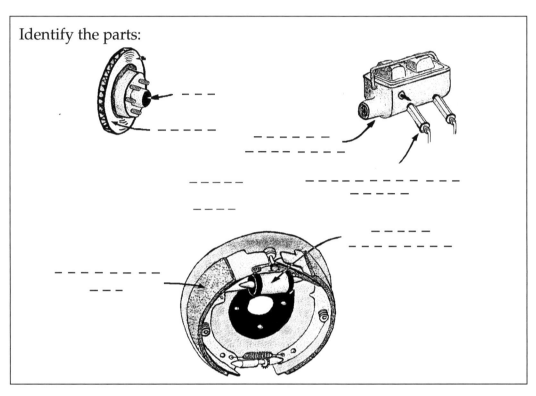

1. Wheel bearings decrease friction, friction pads increase friction. (T) (F) *(p. 67)*

2. Force from a foot pedal is transferred to the wheels using _____fluid. *(p. 64)*

3. A brake pedal is a _____ for a master cylinder. *(p. 64)*

4. Wheel cylinder : _____ *(p. 66)*
   Caliper : Rotor

5. Vehicles often use _____brakes on the front and _____on the rear. *(p. 63)*

6. With ABS, an ECM counts RPMs.(T) or (F) *(p. 68)*

7. Dotted skid marks on a roadway indicates _____. *(p. 68)*

8. The brakes controls how _____, how_____, and how_____ a car slows down. *(p. 63)*

9. Vibrations occur only as the brakes are applied, what's wrong?_____ *(p. 65)*

10. Loud screeching when the brakes are applied indicates_____. *(p. 65)*

11. What will happen if friction pads get wet?_____ *(p. 67)*

12. When brakes are applied, a car skids and swerves to the left. Explain._____
    _____

CHAPTER SEVEN

Electrical System

An automotive *electric system* is a collection of circular electrical pathways. Each pathway, called a *circuit*, includes a wire leading from a *battery*, to an electrical accessory, and then back to the battery. Each accessory has its own circuit, though most circuits share pathways. For example, many circuits use a car's frame as the "wire" for returning electricity to a battery. This return path, commonly called the *ground*, always connects to the *negative battery terminal*.

Circuits vary in their function, location, and physical size. Large wires lead from a battery to a *starter motor,* while almost microscopic wires make-up the *integrated circuits* of computers.

Some circuits are always active, such as, headlights, car alarms, clocks, radio station memory, and seat position memory. Other circuits receive current only when the ignition key is in the "on" position, such as, the radio, power windows, and fan. The *starting circuit* works only when the key is twisted to the "start" position. Other circuits operate only when an engine runs, for instance, the *charging circuit*.

If an electrical pathway breaks, current flow stops, and the accessory will not work. It is not enough for current to reach an accessory; it must also flow through it, and return to the negative battery terminal.

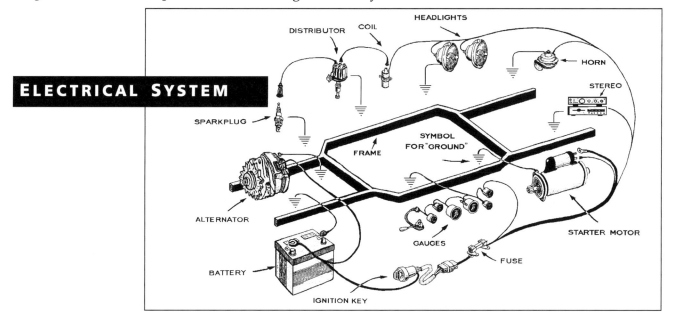

ELECTRICAL SYSTEM

Battery

All automotive circuits use a *battery* as the power source. The main job of a battery is to start an engine. Once running, an engine generates enough electricity to supply itself and all other accessories.

Batteries have two separate sides, the *positive* (+) and *negative* (-). Inside a battery, metal plates, one positive and one negative, are suspended in a liquid *electrolyte*. The electrolyte allows electrons to flow between the two plates without the plates ever touching. Electrons must travel through the electrolyte, usually sulfuric acid, to complete a circuit. The illustration below shows only two plates; in an actual battery, these plates are very close together and are carefully arranged to fill the entire inside of a battery.

A battery works by maintaining a difference between the concentration of electrons contained in these metal plates. This difference produces, in effect, a downhill flow of electrons through a circuit. It is common practice to describe this electron flow as moving from the *positive terminal*, to an accessory, and then back again to the *negative terminal*, or ground.

A large wire (often red) connects between the positive terminal and the starter motor. An equally large wire (almost always black) connects the negative terminal to a car frame. Smaller wires, *insulated* from the frame, branch from the positive terminal to supply all accessories with electric power.

Two types of connections are used with automotive batteries, the *post* variety and a screw-in *side terminal* type. Some batteries offer built-in voltage indicators, some have *filler caps* for adding electrolyte.

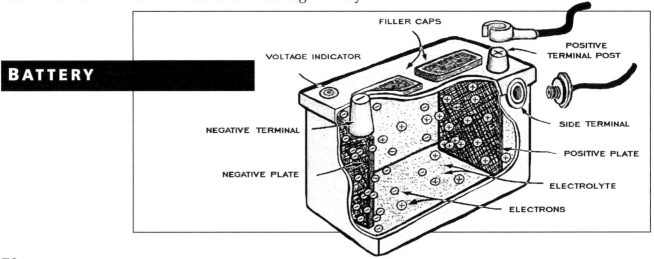

BATTERY

FILLER CAPS

VOLTAGE INDICATOR

POSITIVE TERMINAL POST

NEGATIVE TERMINAL

SIDE TERMINAL

NEGATIVE PLATE

POSITIVE PLATE

ELECTROLYTE

ELECTRONS

Starting Circuit

A *starting circuit,* with the help of gears, a flywheel, and *starter motor,* rotates an engine on electrical power alone until it can start and run by itself. This job requires more electric power than all the other accessories.

When an *ignition key* turns to the "start" position, a small electric current is sent to a *starter solenoid.* A *solenoid* is an electromagnetic switch, separating and protecting the small wires in an ignition key circuit from the huge electric loads used by a starter motor. The solenoid acts as a gate, allowing large amounts of current to flow through a starter motor. A starter solenoid is often attached to the top of a starter motor.

Before electric starter motors, engines had to be started with a hand-crank at the front of a car, attached directly to the crankshaft. This was difficult and dangerous. The electric starter motor, more than anything else, opened motoring to the average person.

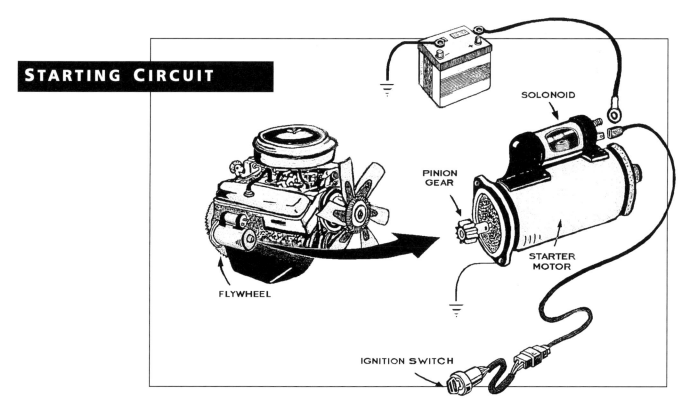

STARTING CIRCUIT

SOLONOID

PINION GEAR

STARTER MOTOR

FLYWHEEL

IGNITION SWITCH

Ignition Circuit

An *ignition circuit* delivers sparks to the combustion chambers. Spark *timing* must be precisely coordinated with the workings of an engine for proper engine performance.

A *distributor* synchronizes spark timing. As an engine turns, a *rotor*, under the *distributor cap*, spins in coordination with internal engine parts. As it spins, the metal tip of a rotor touches each *sparkplug wire*, one after the other. Sparkplug wires are attached in a circle around the outside of the distributor cap and extend through the cap to provide direct contact with a rotor tip. When contact is made, a charge of high voltage current is sent out to individual *sparkplugs*. This particular sequence is called the *firing order* of an engine.

Sparkplugs screw directly through an engine head, with one sparkplug extending into each combustion chamber. When current is sent to a sparkplug, the current must jump the *gap* between the two *electrodes* to complete the circuit. A spark is created when electric current jumps this gap.

A *coil* changes the regular 12 volts from a battery into the 50,000 volts necessary for electric current to jump a sparkplug gap. Mechanical *points*, or in modern cars, an *electronic ignition module*, located inside a distributor cap, manage these different currents, as well as control spark timing.

The type of plug, the voltage delivered, and the size of the sparkplug gap determine the size and temperature of a spark. The size and temperature of a spark controls the speed and burn pattern in a combustion chamber. A single sparkplug will fire approximately 15 times a second with average driving, this equals about one million sparks every 1,000 miles.

IGNITION CIRCUIT

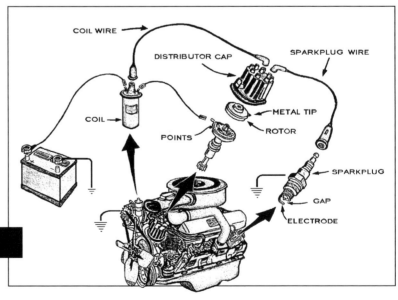

COIL WIRE
DISTRIBUTOR CAP
SPARKPLUG WIRE
COIL
POINTS
METAL TIP
ROTOR
SPARKPLUG
GAP
ELECTRODE

Charging Circuit

A *charging circuit* generates enough electricity to supply a car and all its accessories with electricity. This circuit also *charges*, or replaces, electricity lost from a battery when a car starts.

An *alternator* generates electricity the same way as dams and windmills, by rotating electromagnetic fields. In an automotive charging system, a drive belt from the crankshaft rotates electromagnets inside an alternator to create electric current.

A *voltage regulator* controls the electric current produced by an alter-nator. The faster an engine runs, the more current is produced. At high speed, enough electricity is generated by an alternator to overcharge a battery and to damage the fragile circuits in a vehicle. A voltage regulator limits this current and distributes the right amount of current to the accessories, including the battery.

Modern voltage regulators are electronic and built into an alternator. Older, *mechanical voltage regulators*, are often located to the side of an engine compartment.

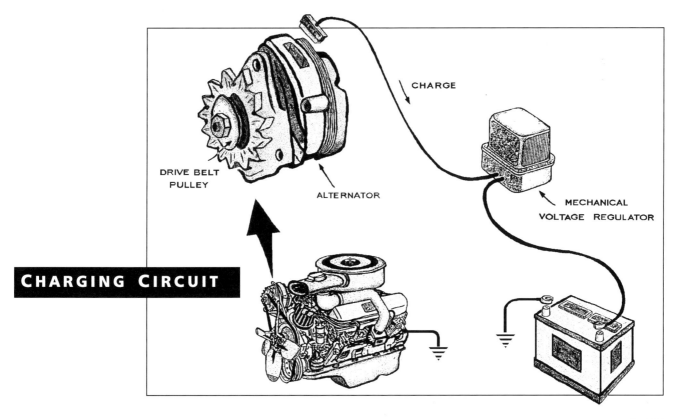

CHARGE

DRIVE BELT
PULLEY

ALTERNATOR

MECHANICAL
VOLTAGE REGULATOR

CHARGING CIRCUIT

Fuses

A *fuse* is a thin metal strip that melts if excessive current is drawn through. Fragile circuits have very thin wire strips as fuses; circuits that require larger electric loads use correspondingly larger wires as fuses. When a fuse melts, the circuit breaks and current flow stops or *shorts*. This protects circuits from damage caused from excess current and provides a built-in and easily replaceable weakest link for a circuit. Most fuses are found in *fuse boxes* located underneath a dashboard.

A *circuit breaker* is a reusable fuse. Rather than melting when overloaded, it expands, physically separating two metal strips. When cooled, a circuit breaker shrinks back, reconnecting the circuit. Some circuit breakers need to be reset by hand. In other circuits, such as the headlight circuit, a circuit breaker automatically resets itself, reestablishing night visibility as soon as possible if a headlight shorts-out while driving.

Fusible links add further protection to major electrical circuits if catastrophic electric failure occurs. When a fusible link melts, some basic circuitry may be saved, but a new fusible link(s) and often significant sections of the wiring must be replaced, to eliminate the original problem.

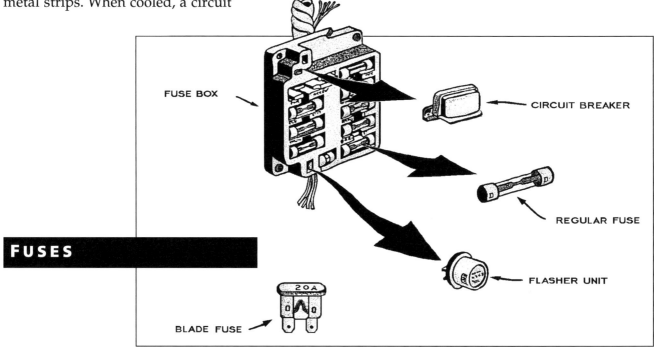

FUSES

FUSE BOX

CIRCUIT BREAKER

REGULAR FUSE

FLASHER UNIT

BLADE FUSE

20A

Accessories

Electrical *accessories* include the many devices that make motoring a little more comfortable, safe, and fun. From windshield wipers to satellite navigation and infrared *night-vision*, automotive gadgetry is both practical and on the cutting edge of technology.

A simple *schematic wiring diagram*, from the author's vintage 1964 British MGB is shown below. Studying this diagram serves as an introduction to the complex diagrams of today's vehicles.

Even the basic incandescent light bulb, used for all the lighting in the diagram below, has been replaced. For example, halogen, or HID (high intensity discharge) bulbs are now used in most headlamps, tail lights, and emergency lights. Instrument panel and applique lights use liquid crystal displays (LCD), light emitting diodes (LED), vacuum florescent displays (VFD), and neon gas lighting.

The ultimate electric accessory, of course, is the electric engine.

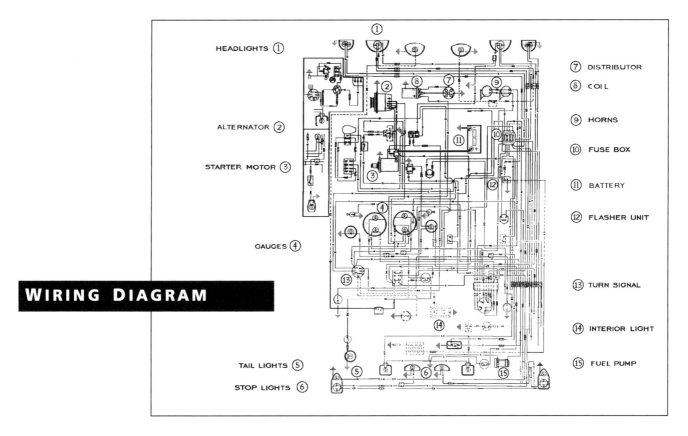

WIRING DIAGRAM

HEADLIGHTS ①

ALTERNATOR ②

STARTER MOTOR ③

GAUGES ④

TAIL LIGHTS ⑤

STOP LIGHTS ⑥

⑦ DISTRIBUTOR

⑧ COIL

⑨ HORNS

⑩ FUSE BOX

⑪ BATTERY

⑫ FLASHER UNIT

⑬ TURN SIGNAL

⑭ INTERIOR LIGHT

⑮ FUEL PUMP

ELECTRICAL TEST

Identify the parts:

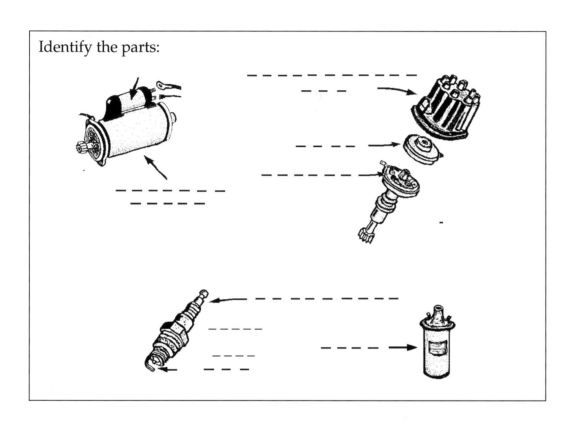

1. The liquid inside a battery is called
   _____. (p. 72)

2. An_____ generates electricity. (p.75)

3. Electric current flows from the _____
   terminal to the_____ terminal. (p. 72)

4. An automotive coil transforms 12 volts
   into _____volts. (p. 74)

5. High voltage is necessary for electricity to
   _____ a sparkplug gap. (p. 74)

6. Sparkplugs extend into the

   _____   _____.

   (p. 9)

7. In cars, a "ground" is also considered the
   _____ battery terminal. (p. 71)

8. The pinion gear of a starter motor meshes
   with the gears of a _____. (p. 73)

9. What creates the heat that melts a fuse?

   _____

10. The radio works but the engine will not
    turn-over. This suggests?_____

    _____

Gaskets

Gaskets prevent leaks between the connecting surfaces of many car parts. Gaskets are made of cork, copper, rubber, thick paper, or various combinations of these materials. When bolted down and squeezed between two surfaces, a gasket fills in gaps. If squeezed too tight, a gasket can be distorted and pushed out of position, causing a leak.

A complex metal and fiber *head gasket* is used between a block and a cylinder head. Cork gaskets are often used for *valve covers* and the *oil pan* or *crankcase*. Thick fiber and paper gaskets are usually used with *water pumps* and *carburetors*. Circular rubber gaskets are found on most *oil filters*. Asbestos and fiber gaskets are used for exhaust manifolds and flange gaskets.

GASKETS

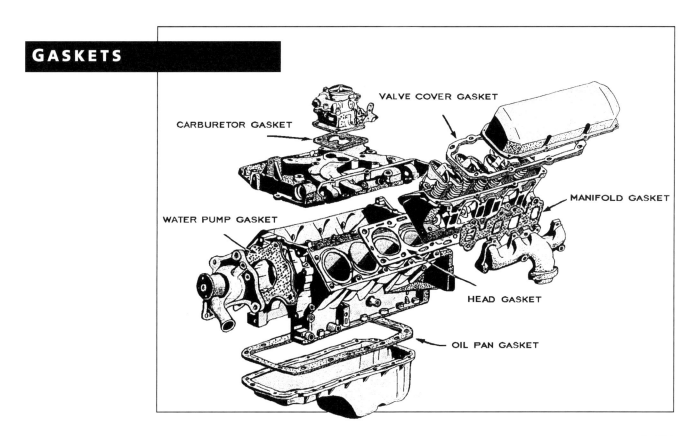

CARBURETOR GASKET
VALVE COVER GASKET
WATER PUMP GASKET
MANIFOLD GASKET
HEAD GASKET
OIL PAN GASKET

Air Conditioning

An air conditioning system uses the same principles of cooling as a home refrigerator. A liquid *refrigerant* circulates in a closed system. A *compressor pump* pressurizes this refrigerant, changing its boiling point, and causing it to vaporize. A radiator, or *condenser*, located in the front of a vehicle, cools the circulating vapor, changing it back to a liquid. This cycle of changing back and forth from liquid to vapor maximizes the amount of heat absorbed. A second radiator, an *evaporator*, becomes cold during this process and air blown over its cool fins is then directed into the passenger compartment through larger pipes called ducts.

An *expansion valve* controls refrigerant pressure, boiling point, and volume. A *sight glass* is used to observe the number of vapor bubbles that remain in the liquid refrigerant as it leaves a condenser. The number of bubbles indicates the volume of refrigerant.

Many other devices are associated with this system, including: check valve, oil bleed line, capillary tube, suction throttle valve, equalizer line, and receiver-dehydrator. Usually automobile air conditioning systems share the same blower, air ducts, and vents with the heater.

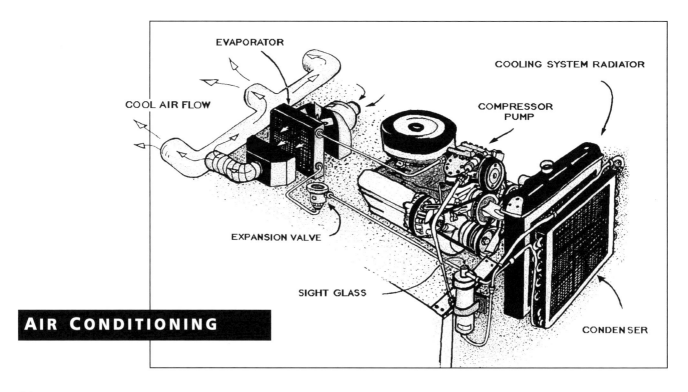

EVAPORATOR

COOLING SYSTEM RADIATOR

COOL AIR FLOW

COMPRESSOR PUMP

EXPANSION VALVE

SIGHT GLASS

CONDENSER

AIR CONDITIONING

APPENDIX C
Safety Tips

1. Drive sensibly, courteously, and soberly

2. Use seat belts (lap and shoulder)

3. Drive a well-maintained car

4. Clean windows and mirrors often

5. Drive a car with air bags

6. Choose a car with ABS brakes

7. Drive in a middle lane of the freeway when possible

8. Drive with the traffic flow

9. Think ahead and look behind, use the rear view mirrors often

10. Carry a safety kit in your car trunk (flashlight, flares, tire inflator, etc.)

11. Carry a cell phone for emergencies, but please don't talk while driving

12. Stop at stoplights and stop signs a few feet back from the crosswalks

13. Join the AAA car club in your area

14. Anticipate trouble from all directions

15. Take road rage to a gym

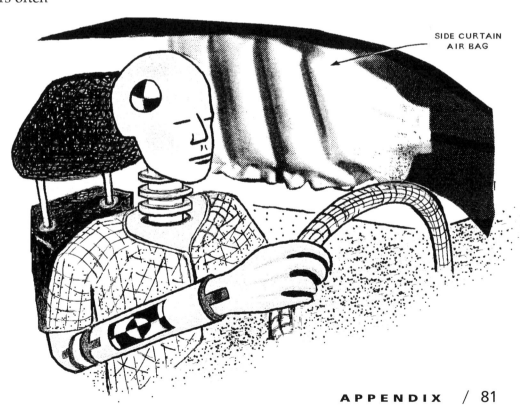

SIDE CURTAIN AIR BAG

Money Saving Tips

1. Start with a good car, then work to improve it

2. Learn **How Cars Work** and then work on them

3. Locate a competent mechanic by word of mouth, not local advertising

4. Tune a car to use the lowest octane gasoline possible

5. Avoid unnecessary idling, turn off an engine while waiting in long lines

6. Keep tires inflated to maximum pressure

7. Rotate tires and change engine oil every 3,000 miles

8. Avoid fast starts and stops

9. Drive slower than you think you should

10. Don't pass highway patrol cars or make eye contact with police officers while driving

GLOSSARY

A

Accelerator—Foot pedal to control engine speed.

Accelerator Pump—Device inside a carburetor that delivers a rapid supply of gasoline to the cylinders.

Accessories—Optional extras for a car: radio, heater, satellite navigation.

Advance—Moving the time when a combustion chamber receives a spark forward, or sooner.

Air Cleaner (Air Filter)—Device that cleans or filters the outside air before it enters a carburetor or fuel injection system.

Air Cooled Engine—Although most engines are cooled by water, a few (mainly Volkswagens) are cooled by outside air drawn in by a cooling fan and forced over the outside of the cylinders.

Air Dam—Device placed under front bumper to reduce air turbulence and drag.

Air Foil—Upside down airplane wing mounted on the trunk of a vehicle to force the rear end of a car downward, increasing the size of the tire tread patch and increasing traction.

Air/Fuel mixture—Ratio of air and gasoline created by a carburetor or fuel injector.

Air Pump—Part of an emission control system that pumps fresh air into an exhaust manifold to increase burning of harmful hydrocarbons.

Alignment—Job done on the front suspension and steering system to point both front tires perfectly straight ahead.

All Wheel Drive (AWD)—A full time 4 wheel drive system.

Alternator—Electrical generator turned by an engine.

Altitude Compensating Modulator (ACM)—Device to control transmission shift spacing and engine timing. Improves performance at higher altitudes by modifying vacuum signals.

Ambient Temperature—Surrounding air temperature.

Ammeter—Meter which measures the rate of current flow through a circuit and shows it on a dashboard gauge, light, or meter.

Amperes (Amps)—Units of measurement used for electrical current flow.

Annulus—An outer ring.

Antifreeze—Petroleum or alcohol based liquid added to the water in a car's radiator to keep it from freezing in cold temperatures.

Anti-BFV—Anti-backfire valve.

Anti-lock Brakes (ABS)—Computerized brake system where a locked brake will be quickly released, thus facilitating stopping.

API—American Petroleum Institute.

Armature—Part used inside generators, starters, and regulators moved by magnetic attraction.

Automatic Transmission—Device that transfers the power produced by an engine to the rear wheels and also gives the driver control over an engine's power.

Automatic Transmission Fluid (ATF)—Low viscosity, high detergent oil-based liquid used to lubricate the internal parts of an automatic transmission.

AutoStick—Modern transmission that can be driven in either manual or automatic shifting style.

Axle—A rod of steel that connects to the center of a wheel and provides the point around which a wheel rotates. In cars, this rod often connects to and transfers power from a differential to a wheel assembly.

B

Backfire—Loud popping noise often the result of a poorly timed engine.

Backfire Suppressor Valve (BSV)—Device used in conjunction with the early design thermactor exhaust emission system. Its primary function is to lean-out the excessively rich fuel mixture which follows closing of a throttle after acceleration.

Backing Plate—In a braking system, the outer ends of axles where brake linings and wheel cylinders are attached.

Backup Lights—White lights at the rear of a car that turn on automatically when a gear selector is placed in reverse, lighting the way when backing-up.

Baffle—Device used to slow or obstruct the flow of gases, liquids, sounds, etc.

Bakelite—Very hard, black or brown plastic-like material used for some automotive parts: for example, a distributor cap.

Balancing—Process of placing weights on the circumference of wheel rims to provide accurate balance for the rim and tire, thus providing a smooth, even ride. Balancing is also used on drive shafts and crankshafts.

Ball and Trunion—Type of universal joint.

Ball Joint—Flexible joint using ball and socket construction in steering and suspension systems.

Barometric and Manifold Absolute Pressure Sensor (BMAP)—A sensor that monitors engine vacuum and barometric pressure to provide engine load information used to calculate spark advance, EGR flow, and air/fuel mixture.

Barometric Pressure Sensor (BARO)—Active sensor (one half of BMAP sensor). Sensor signal is proportional to the Barometric Pressure of the sensor location.

Barrel—Opening in a carburetor through which an air/fuel mixture enters an intake manifold.

Base Circle—Flat area of a camshaft directly opposite the lobe.

Battery—Device for storing and making electricity.

Battery Acid—Liquid or gel electrolyte inside each battery cell.

Battery Cables—Large wires that attach to each terminal of a battery. One is positive and carries current to the engine electrical system and the other cable is negative and grounds the system to the engine and frame of a vehicle.

Battery Charging—Process of replacing electricity in a battery. In a car, this replacement or recharging is done by an alternator.

Battery Posts—Terminals of a battery to which the two large electrical cables are attached.

Bearings—Wear-resistant metal support for a turning shaft. For example: crankshaft and camshaft bearings.

Bell Housing—A large round metal part, attached to the back of an engine, that houses and protects a clutch mechanism.

Bevel—An angle, usually on a gear.

Bias-Ply—Method of tire construction characterized by crisscrossing plies of rubber

Bimetallic Spring—Spring, or metal strip, made of two different metals attached to each other.When heated the different metals expand and contract at different rates, causing the spring to bend.

Bimetal Heat Sensor (BHS)—Unit using a metallic part consisting of 2 layers with different metals, to sense temperature changes. The layers expand at different rates as temperature changes causing the part to bend in a pre-determined manner, thereby causing a changing signal as a function of temperature..

Bleeding—Process of removing air bubbles from the fluid in a hydraulic brake system.

Block—Most fundamental and heaviest part of an engine.

Blow-By—Combustion and vapor leakage past the piston rings and into a crankcase causing loss of power.

Blower Motor—Electrical motor that blows or forces air through a heater, defroster, or air conditioner and into a passenger compartment.

Blueprinting—Rebuilding an engine to exact specifications.

Body—External, enclosing part of the car: roof, fenders, doors, floor, hood, trunk.

Bog—Expression used to describe an engine condition where, as a throttle is opened, engine power drops rather than increases.

Bolts—A bolt is the part with threads on its outside that a nut screws onto or over.

Boots—Generally means rubber covers that protect CV joints and certain steering parts.

Bore and Stroke—Bore is the diameter of one engine cylinder; the stroke is the distance one piston travels up and down. These figures are often seen together, measured in inches or cm: for example, 3.680 x 3.130 in.

Boss—Heavy cast section used for support, such as the heavy section around a bearing.

Bowl—Rounded compartment in a carburetor containing a specified level of gasoline.

Bypass Valve (BPV)—Vacuum controlled valve in the Thermactor system which allows air from the air pump to be injected into the exhaust system or bypassed to the atmosphere when not required; and also provides a pressure relief function to protect the air pump from high pressures.

Brakes—The system and its components used to stop car.

Brake Fluid—Hydraulic fluid used to maintain pressure in either a disc or drum brake system.

Brake Lines—Conductor tubing system which contains and carries brake fluid throughout the system.

Brake Lights—When the brake pedal is pressed, the taillights (or brake lights) are switched on to warn following cars that you are stopping.

Disc Brakes—Brake system using pads pinching against a disc or rotor.

Drum Brakes—Brake system that uses shoes that expand outward and press against a drum.

Hand Brake—*(see parking brake)*

Power Brakes—Either a disc or drum brake system with a powered assistance to brake pedal application.

Self-adjusting Brakes—Brakes that keep themselves in adjustment by resetting when brakes are applied while backing.

Breaker Points—(see points)

Break-In—Gradually wearing-in or acclimating a new engine to running conditions.

Breather—Vent on a valve cover which allows fumes to escape from a crankcase. On older cars these fumes escaped into the atmosphere: on newer cars they are recirculated and burned in an engine. In either case, they still exit through a breather.

Bucket Seats—Individual passenger seats that conform to or surround the body more than flat or bench seats.

Bumpers—Heavy rubber or chrome pieces on the extreme front and rear of a car designed to absorb shocks in an accident.

Bushing—Spacing device similar to a bearing, usually applied to smaller shafts with smaller loads.

Butterfly Nut—A nut with a butterfly "wings" for easy turning. Also know as a wing nut.

Butterfly Valve—(see throttle)

Bypass—To go around some restriction such as a thermostat, valve, switch, circuit, or water pump, etc.

C

Cable—Heavily insulated large diameter wire such as a battery cable or a spark plug cable.

Camber—Outward tilt of the tops of the front wheels so when loaded and moving forward, the tendency to tilt inward will cause them to become correctly vertical.

Camshaft (Cam)—Raised or flattened section on a rotating shaft used to provide a timed mechanical sequence or movement. As a crankshaft turns inside an engine, it turns another, smaller shaft, which opens and closes the valves.

Canister—Enclosed can containing activated charcoal or carbon. Used to absorb unburned hydrocarbon vapors from a gas tank and fuel system. Often located in an engine compartment.

CANP (Canister Purge Solenoid)—Electrical solenoid that opens valve from fuel vapor canister line to an intake manifold. This controls flow of vapors between tank, carburetor bowl vent, and carbon canister when an engine is running.

Capacity--Maximum amount of material held by a container or system.

Carbon Monoxide (CO)—Poisonous, gaseous by-product of engine combustion, odor less and color less.

Cardan Joint—Type of universal joint.

Caster--Slight backward tilt of the center axis of the front wheels, like a caster on furniture legs. Part of the process of wheel alignment

Catalytic Converter—Muffler-like device located in an exhaust system where hot exhaust gas comes in contact with special metals (platinum or palladium) that promote more complete combustion of unburned hydrocarbons and a conversion of some emissions.

Cavitation—Space created at the center of a rotating pump when it does not fill as fast as the fluid is pumped out.

CFI (Central Fuel Injection)—Computer controlled fuel injection system using two fuel injectors and a divided throttle body.

Chassis—An automobile frame with an engine and all running parts in place but without a body, interior, trim and accessories.

Check Valve—One-way valve which allows a liquid or gas to flow in only one direction.

Choke—System, either manual or automatic, that richens an air/fuel mixture to make a newly started or cold engine run smoother.

Chuggle—Jarring sensation common to late-model cars with "lock-up" torque converters in the automatic transmission.

Circuit—Course that an electrical current takes. For example, from the positive battery terminal, to the headlights and then back to the negative battery terminal would be a complete circuit.

Circuit Breaker—Fuse-like device that can be reset without replacement.

Clearance—Very small space separating two moving parts.

Clutch—Mechanical or hydraulic device which momentarily disconnects a spinning engine from the transmission gears so that other gears can be engaged by the gear shifting lever.

Cog—A tooth on a gear.

Coil—Electrical transformer which increases low current to a high voltage.

Cold Start Spark Advance System—Added to a distributor spark control to regulate distributor spark advance, used when engine coolant temperature is below 128 degrees F.

Cold Start Spark Hold System—Provides improved cold engine acceleration when engine coolant is less than 128 degrees F.

Cold Weather Modulator—Vacuum modulator located in some carburetor air cleaners. Prevents the air cleaner duct door from opening to non-heated intake air when fresh air is below 55 degrees F.

Combustion—A controlled burning or explosion within a combustion chamber caused by igniting a gaseous vapor with a spark.

Components—Parts that make up a system.

Compression—Maximum pressure produced on an air/fuel mixture in a combustion chamber when a piston moves up to the top of its stroke.

Compression Gauge—Measuring device inserted into a spark plug hole to measure the amount of compression produced in a chamber, indicating of the degree of seal provided by the valves and piston rings.

Compression Ratio—The amount of pressure created in a combustion chamber as a function of the degree of seal and volume of the combustion chamber.

Compressor—Part of an air conditioning system that condenses the freon gas in the system.

Condensation—Changing gas vapor to liquid by cooling (steam to water).

Condenser—Component of an ignition system (in a distributor) which prevents the arcing of electrical current across the contact surfaces of the points. Also, called a capacitor.

Conductor—Material capable of transferring electric current.

Connecting Rod (Con Rod)—Device that connects a piston to a crankshaft.

Console—Decorative and functional box between bucket seats, sometimes extending to the dashboard.

Contact Set—(see points)

Continuously Variable Transmission (CVT)—Modern transmission with "seamless" electronically controlled shifting.

Control Arm—Part of a suspension and steering system that connects the wheel.

Coolant—Water and antifreeze mixture in a cooling system.

Cooling System—Process by which coolant is circulated inside an engine and through a radiator to absorb heat and then disperse it to the surrounding air flow.

Cotter Pin—Bent wire clip pushed through a hole in the end of a bolt to prevent it from accidently unscrewing. A safety device used on wheels, steering, and suspension systems.

Coupling—Connecting device used to transfer motion.

Crankcase—Bottom most part of an engine where the crankshaft is housed and engine oil is stored.

Cranking—Turning an engine over with the starter motor via the ignition key.

Crankshaft—Heavy shaft at the bottom of an engine that converts the up and down piston motion into spinning motion.

Crankshaft Position Sensor—Permanent magnet, with coil, that provides RPM information used to calculate spark advance, EGR flow, and air/fuel ratio.

Cupping—Depressions or cup-shaped wear patterns on a tire due to misalignment.

Current—Movement of electricity through wires or through a whole circuit.

Cylinder—Large hole in an engine block where a piston fits and travels up and down.

Cylinder Head—Engine component that provides small indentations for the combustion chambers and a cover for the cylinders. A head on most engines provides holes for the spark plugs and valve assemblies.

Constant-Velocity (CV) joints—Heavy duty, highly flexible, universal joint used for high load and high movement conditions.

D

Damper—Device to remove or reduce vibration oscillation, etc.

Dashboard—Front part of a passenger compartment, located under the windshield. Contains the instrument cluster, radio, glove compartment, etc.

Dashpot—Chamber used to slow or dampen movement, usually for low load use.

Decel Fuel Shutoff—Gas saving device to shut off excess gas flow to a carburetor following sudden decreases in engine speed.

Defroster—Part of the cooling system that blows hot air onto the inside of a windshield to eliminate and prevent window steaming.

DEFI (digital electronic fuel injection)—Computerized fuel injection system.

Detonation—Knocking sound caused by the premature burning of an air/fuel mixture in a combustion chamber. (see pre-ignition)

Dieseling—Condition where an engine continues to run after the key is turned off. Often the result of carbon build-ups on the tops of pistons. These build-ups, or hot spots, retain enough heat to ignite an air/fuel mixture.

Differential—Part in the center of the rear axles where a gear arrangement allows spin force to be directed to the rear wheel assemblies.

Discs—(see brakes)

Dimmer—Steering column or floor switch used to change headlight beams from low to high beam.

Dipstick—Flat metal rod used to measure the amount of fluid in an engine, transmission, or power steering unit.

Displacement—Maximum volume possible for all the combustion chambers.

Distributor—Ignition system device that delivers the high voltage current from a coil to the spark plugs.

Distributor Cables—Heavy wires which conduct high voltage current from a coil to the spark plugs via the distributor. Also called spark plug cables, or spark plug wires.

Distributor Cap—Black bakelite cover for the top of a distributor, to which the spark plug cables connect.

Distributor Rotor—Uppermost internal part of a distributor. This mechanism rotates with an engine and directs high voltage electricity to the proper spark plugs.

DOHC—Double over-head camshaft.

D.O.T.—Department of Transportation.

Drive belt—Steel reinforced rubber belt formed in a "V" to fit the groove of a pulley. The belt transfers spin power from one pulley to another.

Driveshaft—Long hollow shaft turned by a transmission which in turn transmits spinning power to the rear wheels via a differential.

Drum—(see brakes)

Dwell Angle—Number of degrees that a distributor shaft rotates between openings of the points.

Dwell Meter—Gauge to measure dwell angle, used to time an ignition system.

Dynamic Response Test (DRT)—Engine test where a rapid acceleration is applied to an engine and the engine is checked for appropriate throttle movement, rate of change in rpm, and change in the intake air flow.

E

Eccentric—Shape made when one circle is superimposed on a second circle with each circle having a different center.

Electronic Control Assembly (ECA)—Vehicle computer consisting of a calibration assembly containing the computer memory, control program, and a CPU.

Electronic Control Module (ECM)—Electronic center piece of a computerized system.

Engine Coolant Temperature Sensor (ECT)--Refers to thermistor sensor immersed in engine coolant fluid and used to provide engine coolant temperature information which is used to alter spark advance and EGR flow during warm-up or overheating conditions.

Electronic Engine Control (EEC)—Computer directed system of engine control.(see ECA)

Evaporative Emission Shed System (EESS)—System for containment of evaporated fuel vapors from gasoline tank and fuel systems.

Electronic Fuel Injection (EFI)—System of computer controlled fuel injection, usually using one or two injectors placed in an intake manifold.

Exhaust Gas Check (EGC) Valve—Device that allows air to enter an exhaust manifold but prevents reverse flow in event of improper operation of other components.

Exhaust Gas Oxygen Sensor (EGO)— S
This sensor changes its output voltage as exhaust gas oxygen content changes.

Exhaust Gas Recirculation (EGR)—Procedure where a small amount of exhaust gas is readmitted to the combustion chamber to reduce peak combustion temperatures and thus reduce NOx emissions.

Electrode—Two terminals in an electrical system that are separated by a gap which the current must jump, ie. the electrode tip of a spark plug.

Electrolyte—Liquid inside an automotive battery which is composed of about 60% water and 40% sulfuric acid.

Electronic scattershield (governor circuit)—Device to cut out fuel or ignition if a preset speed is exceeded under certain conditions. Mazda RX-7's, for example, cannot be over-revved because of an electronic safeguard.

Electronic Spark Control System (ESC)—Electronic distributor vacuum control system aiding in more complete combustion through controlled spark retard under certain temperature and speed conditions.

Emissions—Gaseous compounds expelled from a car's crankcase, exhaust, carburetor, and fuel tank (hydrocarbons, nitrogen oxides, and carbon monoxide).

Emission Control Systems—Components used to reduce engine pollutants.

Emergency Brake—(see parking brake)

Engine—Device that creates spinning motion from exploding gasoline fumes.

Engine Mounts—Thick rubber parts used to hold an engine in place yet give it slight flexibility to dampen vibration.

Environmental Protection Agency (EPA) —Federal agency having responsibility for administrating congressional programs relating to the protection of the environment.

Ethyl Gasoline—A chemical added to gasoline to eliminate knocking.

Evaporation—Process of fluid turning into vapor either from heat or exposure to air.

Exhaust Valve Position Sensor (EVP)—Potentiometric sensor that allows ECA to determine actual EGR flow at any point in time.

Exhaust—The by-product or leftovers from the combustion process expelled from an engine.

Exhaust Gas Analyzer—An instrument for determining the amount of HC and CO emitted to the atmosphere. A means of determining the efficiency with which an engine burns fuel.

Exhaust Heat Control Valve—Valve that routes hot exhaust gases to an intake manifold heat riser during cold engine operation The valve can be thermostatically controlled, or vacuum operated.

Exhaust Manifold--Cast iron "funnel" used to collect and expel exhaust fumes. A Manifold funnels the gases into a single pipe that carries them out the tail pipe at the rear of a vehicle.

F

Fading—Condition of brake failure where friction pads lose their stopping ability because of continuous use and over heating.

Feedback Carburetor System (FBC)—system of fuel control employing a computer controlled motor that varies the carburetor air/fuel mixture.

Filter—Device to remove particles from a fluid or gas.

Firewall The partition between

Float—Device supported by fluid. In a carburetor, a float is used to sense fluid level and shut off flow

before overflow occurs.

Flooding—Condition where an engine will not start because the air/fuel mixture is too rich to ignite. Often the result of over pumping a gas pedal.

Floorboard—Floor of a passenger compartment.

Flywheel—Heavy disk of iron with gear teeth along the outer circumference. The gears engage with the smaller pinion gear on a starter motor and the large mass absorbs and smooths wobbles.

Fouling—Build-up of carbon and oily deposits on the electrodes of a sparkplug.

Four- Wheel Drive (4WD)—All four wheels receive engine power.

Frame—Heavy steel skeleton of a car that an engine and all other parts are mounted on.

Friction—The resistance to movement caused by two objects rubbing against each other.

Front Suspension—(see suspension)

Front-Wheel Drive—A car with an engine and drive wheels in the front.

Fuel—Any material that produces heat or power by burning. Gasoline or diesel fuel are the most common fuels for internal combustion engines.

Fuel Decel Valve (FDV)—Valve which, during deceleration, adds fuel to an intake manifold to enrich the air/fuel mixture and provide more complete combustion.

Fuel Pump (FP) Relay—Electrical relay used to supply power to an electric fuel pump of EFI/CFI system

Fuel Control Solenoid (FCS)—Controls the carburetor air/fuel ratio by one of two methods: 1) a pulsating solenoid that bleeds air into the "main" and "idle" fuel system, 2) a solenoid which includes a vacuum regulator/diaphragm that controls fuel flow, in the "main" fuel system and bleeds air into the "idle" fuel system.

Fuel Injection--A method of metering and mixing fuel with air and then accurately timing its injection into the cylinders. Fuel injection is used instead of a carbureted fuel system.

Fuel Pump—Mechanical or electrical device used to bring gasoline from a tank to a carburetor or fuel injection system.

Fuel Tank—Storage tank where fuel is held before being pumped to a carburetor or fuel injectors.

Fuel-Vacuum Separator—Used to filter waxy hydrocarbons from carburetor ported vacuum lines. This protects the vacuum delay valve and other vacuum controlled devices.

Fumes—Gaseous vapors.

Fuse—A protective device that acts as the "weakest link" in an electric circuit. Usually a metal strip in a glass or plastic case which melts and breaks the circuit if a current flow becomes too large.

G

Gasket—Soft, thin material, often paper, fiber, rubber, cork, or copper, used to create a seal between two surfaces. When two surfaces are tightened together with the gasket between them, a gasket will fill-in any gaps or scars that may leak.

Gasoline—A highly flammable hydrocarbon, petroleum-based fuel used mainly as an automotive fuel.

Gauges—Tool or instrument for measuring gaps, thicknesses, pressures, etc.

Gear Ratio—Number of teeth on one gear compared to the number of teeth on a meshing gear. If a gear having ten teeth is meshed with a gear having thirty teeth, the gear ratio is one to three. So, if the smaller gear turns completely around once, the larger gear will be turned around one-third of a full rotation.

Gear Shift—Lever inside a passenger compartment used to select and change transmission gears.

Generator—Device for generating electricity. Called an alternator in cars.

Glow Plug--Special glowing sparkplug used to start diesel engines.

Grabbing—Brake problem characterized by the brakes overreacting to pedal pressure or pulling to the side when pedal is applied.

Ground (GND)—Electrical term indicating a return path for electricity or a functionally infinite amount of capacity for receiving electric currant, as in the earth (ground) itself. In a vehicle the frame and engine serve as a ground and are also connected to the negative terminal of a car battery.

H

Half Shaft—Solid steel rod extending from front wheel drive transaxle to the center of a wheel assembly. Counter part of drive shaft.

Hair Spring— A very fine spring, coiled in a flat plane so the diameter of the spring keeps expanding as it is wound.

Halon—Type of gas used in new fire extinguishes. Excellent for putting out fires without damaging neighboring components.

Handbrake—(see parking brake)

Header—A high performance exhaust manifold system, offering less restriction to escaping exhaust gases, which increases power.

Head—(see cylinder head)

Heater—Small radiator connected to the cooling system that disperses engine heat on demand into a passenger compartment. This system is also used to supply heat to the windshield defroster.

Heat Riser—Valve in an exhaust pipe that directs exhaust gases against the outer surface of an intake manifold. This helps heat a carburetor and air/fuel mixture faster.

High Voltage wires—Spark plug wires that run from a distributor cap to the spark plugs.

Hydrocarbon (HC)—Any compound composed of carbon and hydrogen, such as petroleum products. Excessive amounts in the atmosphere are considered undesirable contaminants.

Hood—Part of a car's body that opens and closes to provide access to an engine compartment.

Horsepower—Unit of measurement to rate engine power, its ability to do work. Historically horsepower is the ability of one horse to lift 33,000 pounds one foot in one minute. Many refined definitions are now used to measure horsepower, ie. frictional, gross, net, braking, and indicated horsepower.

Hoses—Rubber and plastic tubes that carry either water in a cooling system, air in a vacuum system, fluid in a hydraulic system, oil in the lubrication system, fuel in the fuel system, or freon in an air-conditioning system.

Hot Idle Compensator (HIC)—Thermostatically controlled carburetor valve that opens when input air temperatures are high. Additional air is allowed to discharge below the throttle (butterfly) plates at engine idle. This feature improves idle stability and prevents the rich fuel mixture normally associated with increased fuel vaporization caused by a hot engine.

Hub—Center part of a wheel assembly that houses the wheel bearings.

Hybrid engines—The combining of gas and electric engines in the same vehicle.

Hydraulics—Any process that uses the force of a compressed liquid to effect a mechanical reaction.

Hydraulic Brakes—Pressurized liquid linkage in a brake system between a pedal and friction pads. For example, brake fluid under pressure is used to cause an expansion of the brake shoe against a drum.

Hydraulic Valves—System within an engine whereby oil under pressure is used to open and close engine valves.

Hydrocarbons—Hydrocarbons are a by-product of unburned gasoline. They are one of the three main pollutants caused by an automobile and are a result of either gasoline that was not completely burned in the combustion process or of the evaporation of liquid gasoline.

Hydrometer—In automotives, a device that measures specific gravity of battery fluid by the depth that a float sinks into the fluid being tested.

I

Idle—When an engine is running at its lowest speed, just above stalling and usually disconnected from the drive train (Neutral).

Idle Adjustment—Controlling engine idle speed, for example, with an adjustment screw on a carburetor.

Idle Limiter—Device to control minimum and maximum idle fuel richness to a carburetor. Aids in preventing overly tight idle adjustments.

Idle Limiter Caps—Plastic caps over the idle adjustment screws to prevent amateur tampering with the idle and therefore the possible increased emission of pollutants.

Idle Mixture—Mixture ratio of fuel and air used for low idling speed.

Idle Speed Control (ISC)—Actuator mounted to a fuel charging assembly which controls idle speed. The ISC functions at high cam rpm and is driven by an ECA and includes an integral idle tracking switch (ITS).

Idle Tracking Switch (ITS)—Part of an idle speed control motor that determines when a throttle is at idle.

Idle Vacuum Valve—Device used with other vacuum controls to dump air during extended period of idle. Provides protection for a catalytic converter.

Ignition—Process of igniting an air/fuel mixture in the combustion chamber.

Ignition Module Signal (IMS)—Signal produced by the ECA that controls an ignition module's ON and OFF time and therefore the spark timing.

Ignition Pressure Switch Assembly—Pressure switches used on turbocharged engines to retard spark timing during boost times to prevent engine damage.

Ignition System—Parts used to ignite an air/fuel mixture in the combustion chambers. These parts include the battery, ignition switch (key), coil, distributor and spark plugs, as well as all the wires, cables, relays, terminals and associated equipment required.

Inertia Switch—Switch in a fuel pump circuit that shuts off power to a fuel pump in the event a vehicle is involved in a collision. This switch must be manually reset.

Injector—Fuel spraying device using tiny solenoids to regulate spray size and duration.

In-Line Engine—Engine design where cylinders are arranged in a single row.

Impeller—A propeller inside a pump. This rotating part, often rubber, increases the moving speed of fluids and gases.

Instruments—Gauges on a dashboard that monitor a car's vital functions.

Intake Manifold—Passageways and chambers directly under a carburetor or throttle body fuel injection system, where the air/fuel mixture is distributed and waits to be drawn into the combustion chambers.

Internal Combustion Engine—Theory and application of containing an explosion in a closed area and harnessing the resultant power to move a piston which then turns a shaft to provide spinning power.

J

Jet—Small tube or nozzle inside a carburetor through which fuel flows and is thus controlled.

Jumper Cables—Set of large wires and clamps used to connect the battery terminals of one vehicle to another. A car with a dead battery can be started using these cables. If proper procedures are not followed, battery explosions and damage to computer parts can result.

K

Kerosene—Petroleum derivative formerly used as a fuel and now chiefly used as a cleaning solvent.

Kickdown Switch—Commonly called a "passing gear," this is a switch in a carburetor where flooring a gas pedal and fully opening a carburetor causes an automatic transmission to shift down into the next lower gear yielding greater passing power.

Kingpin—A large vertical bolt around which a front wheel turns.

Knock—A tapping or rattling sound in an engine caused by incorrect ignition timing or by loose or worn engine parts such as bearings.

L

Leaf Spring—A method of suspending a car body from an engine, drive train, and frame. This type of spring is used on the rear suspensions of most cars.

Lean Mixture—Too little fuel in an air/fuel mixture. As opposed to a rich mixture.

Limited Slip Differential—A type of driveshaft and rear axle arrangement where if one rear wheel spins freely, the spin force will be transferred to the other rear wheel. This allows one wheel to find traction should the other wheel be spinning in mud or snow.

Limiter—(see idle limiter)

Linings—(see brake linings)

Lobe—High portion of a camshaft.

Lube Job—Usually means injecting grease into the suspension and steering ball joints and/or other fittings. May involve changing engine oil, transmission fluid and/or differential fluid.

Lubricant—A slippery substance, including engine oil and heavy grease.

Lubricating System—The system and parts that hold, pump, distribute, and recirculate oil throughout an engine.

Lug Nuts—The large nuts used to hold a tire and rim to a wheel hub.

M

MacPherson Strut—Special shock absorber that incorporates coil springs and shock absorbers in the same unit.

Mags—Special racing wheel rims often made of magnesium for weight-saving purposes.

Manifold Air Pressure (MAP)—Sensor and computer control system that regulates air/fuel mixture as a function of air pressure.

Main Bearings—Hold and support a crankshaft at the bottom of an engine block.

Manifold—Metal casting of passages that connects and funnels gases and/or fluids either to smaller openings as with the exhaust manifold system or expands the openings, as with an intake manifold system.

Manifold Air Temperature (MAT)—Sensor and computer control system that regulates air/fuel mixture as a function of air temperature.

Mean Effective Pressure—Calculated average pressure in the combustion chamber following combustion.

Misfire—Partial or intermittent non ignition in one or more combustion chambers.

Mixture—Fuel/air ratio created in a carburetor, intake manifold, and combustion chamber.

Muffler—An exhaust system part constructed to dull

the noise created by a running engine.

N

Negative—The "ground" side of a battery or an automotive electrical circuit.

Neutral Drive Switch (BDS)—Used in automatic transmissions to adjust idle speed due to the increased loading of an engaged transmission.

Nipple—Hollow metal connection point over which a hose is attached.

Nitrous Oxide (NOx)--Compound formed during engine combustion process when oxygen in the air combines with nitrogen in the air to form the nitrogen oxides, the agents in photochemical smog. Also used, ironically, as a performance booster, forced into combustion chambers under pressure.

Nut—A nut is a donut-shaped object which is threaded on its inside edge and screws down over the threaded outside of a bolt.

O

Octane—System used to rate fuel according to its volatility or the temperature at which it will ignite. This factor is responsible for delivering antiknock qualities to gasoline.

Ohm—Unit of measurement used to indicate the resistance to current flow in an electrical circuit.

Oil—Any liquid lubricant but chiefly the oil used to lubricate an engine.

Oil Capacity—Volume of oil that an engine's lubricating system requires.

Oil Filter—Replaceable, screw-on, canister that holds a gauzy mesh used to filter and remove solid impurities from a lubricating system.

Oil Pan—Large tank on the bottom of an engine used as a collection and pumping reservoir for a lubricating system.

Oil Pump—Small mechanical device which picks oil up from an oil pan and pumps it to those parts of an engine that need lubrication.

Open Circuit—Circuit that does not provide a complete path for the flow of current, no continuity. (See Short Circuit)

O-rings—Circular rubber rings used as seals.

Out-of-Round—A condition of wear.

Overdrive—Extra high gear for a transmission, used to increase gasoline milage.

Oversteer—Handling condition, common in rear-engine cars, where the greater weight in the back causes the rear end to try to "pass" the front of a car. A vehicle turns too easily.

Oxidation—Chemical combination of a material with oxygen. For example, rust is an oxidation process.

Oxygen sensor—Indicates the amount of oxygen in the exhaust gas, so a computer can make adjustments to the air/fuel mixture and the engine timing. This device looks like a sparkplug but screws into an exhaust manifold, or exhaust pipe, near an engine.

P

Parking Brake—Secondary brake system, either hand or foot operated, used to prevent a car from slipping when parked.

Parking Lights—Small, white or amber lights at the front of a car.

Part Throttle—Engine operating speed between idle and full throttle. Generally considered to be cruising speed.

Petroleum Crude oil—Substance pumped from the ground and then refined into a variety of forms, such as oil, grease,gasoline, kerosene, and plastic.

Ping—Rattling, sharp knocking sound in an engine during acceleration caused by improper timing or by gasoline of too low an octane.

Piston—Soup can shaped device inside a cylinder that is forced downward by the combustion explosion and then turns a crankshaft via a connecting rod.

Piston Rings—Series of spring steel "bracelets" fitted around the upper outside of a piston. The rings push outward against the sides of cylinder walls providing the seal necessary to contain the explosive forces in combustion chambers. Rings also keep the lubricating oil from splashing up, into a combustion chamber, and burning along with the gasoline.

Planetary Gear—Gear set which orbits around and mesh with a central sun gear and ring gear. A planetary gear set is commonly used in a differential.

Play—Amount of movement in a mechanical device. Used when referring to automotive steering and front end operation. Steering wheel play is the amount a wheel can be turned, side-to-side, before the front wheels begin to turn.

Points—Set of electrical contacts inside a distributor that open and close the electrical circuit from a coil to the spark plugs.

Port—Opening through which liquids or gases flow.

Positive Crankcase Ventilation Valve (PCV)—One-way valve that allows recirculation of waste gases from inside an engine crankcase to reburned in the combustion process.

Positive Temperature Coefficient Heater (PTC)—Temperature sensitive electric assisted choke system activated when surrounding temperature is above 60 degrees F. Permits earlier opening of the choke butterfly plates to increase gasoline milage.

Positraction—(see limited slip differential)

Potentiometer (pot)—Variable resistor, or dimmer switch.

Power—Amount of work done in a specific period of time. (See Horsepower)

Power Steering—Hydro-mechanical system where the process of turning the front wheels is made easier. Sometimes called a power assist unit.

Power Train—Parts of an automobile that are related to propelling it, including: an engine, transmission, driveshaft, differential, and rear axle.

Pre-Ignition—Condition when a combustion explosion occurs slightly before the spark plug fires. The cause is related to a poorly timed and tuned engine, or glowing charcoal deposits on piston tops. (see detonation)

Pressure—Force of an external object or substance against something. Also the internal force of a substance created by expansion or compression.

Pressure Cap—*(see radiator cap).*

Profile Ignition Pickup (PIP)—Sensor that sends crankshaft position information to an ECM (main computer).

Pulley—Grooved wheel used to transmit spin power from one source to another using a rubber belt fitted into the groove.

Pulling—Condition where a vehicle swerves to the side when the brakes are applied or if the frame is misaligned.

Pulse Air System—Type of exhaust control system which uses the natural exhaust pulses in a tuned exhaust pipe. A reed-type check valve responds to the negative pressure pulses and permits air to be drawn into an exhaust system.

Push Rod—Solid steel rod between a camshaft lobe and a valve rocker arm. A push rod will push on a rocker arm which in turn will push open a valve.

Push Start—Starting a car by quickly letting a clutch pedal out and then back in, while a vehicle is rolling. The rolling car's energy turns over the engine when the clutch is let out, pushing it in allows a neutral position for better control.

R

Radiator—Large receptacle mounted in front of a vehicle through which coolant circulates to dispense engine heat.

Radiator Cap—Easily removable seal for a radiator. When replaced it seals a radiator so pressure can build up to a predetermined level and then release coolant and steam to maintain that pressure.

Radiator Core—Lower part of a radiator that consists of rows of tubing finned for maximum cooling.

Radiator Hoses—The two, upper and lower, large rubber tubes that connect a radiator to an engine. *(see hoses)*

Recap—Process by which new treads are mounted (melted) onto an old tire casing. With today's high tech tires and small cars this process is largely restricted to commercial users as a cost saving device.

Regulator—*(see voltage regulator)*

Relay—Switching device operated by a low current circuit, that controls the opening and closing of another circuit of higher current capacity.

Relief Valve—A pressure limiting valve that releases fluids or gases to maintain a constant pressure within a system.

Resistance—Electrical term that refers to the ability of a conductor (such as a wire) to oppose or restrict current coming through it. Copper has a low resistance and rubber has high resistance. (see ohms)

Retard—Moving back he time when a combustion chamber receives a spark.

Revolutions Per Minute (rpm)—Refers to the number of times something (a crankshaft) rotates in one minute.

Rich Mixture—Too much fuel in an air/fuel mixture. As opposed to a lean mixture.

Rim—Wheel of a car minus the tire is the rim. *(see mags)*

Rings—*(see piston rings).*

Rotary Engine—Different type of internal combustion engine, one without pistons, connecting rods or a conventional crankshaft.

Rotor—*(see distributor, and brakes)*

S

Sagging—Condition where one or more corners of a vehicle are too low to the ground. Often the result of worn-out springs.

Sealed Beam—Type of light bulb used in auto headlights.

Sending Units—These are the "other ends" of the gauges on the dashboard and the computer control units. For example, a measuring device within an engine determines the oil pressure and sends that information in the form of voltage changes to an oil pressure gauge on a dash. Each electrical gauge has a sending unit of some type.

Serpentine Belt—Exceptionally long and complicated drive belt .(see drive belt)

Set Screw--Small screw used to secure a shaft in a collar. A set screw is tightened or "set" against a shaft to prevent movement between the collar and shaft. Set screws often hold pulleys to shafts.

Sheet Metal—Thin sheets of metal used to make the body or outside surface of a car including the fenders, hood, doors, and trunk.

Shift—To change gears in a transmission.

Shift Indicator Light—System primarily controlled by engine speed and manifold vacuum that provides a visual indication to a driver when to shift to the next higher gear to obtain fuel economy.

Shift Linkage—Mechanisms that connect a shift lever to a transmission.

Shimmy—Vibration caused by misalignment of the front wheels or worn front suspension or steering parts.

Shock Absorber—Hydraulic (fluid-filled) device situated near each wheel which absorbs and dampens road shocks and spring vibrations.

Shoe—(see brakes)

Short Circuit—Path of least current resistance which allows current to take a path other than its designated one, ie., a break in a wire which allows contact with a grounded component.

Shroud—Fiberglass, plastic, or sheet metal hood surrounding a cooling fan. This is a safety device to prevent injury and a way to increase fan efficiency.

SMPI—Electronic sequential multi-port fuel injection.

SOHC—Single over-head camshaft.

Solenoid—Electric switch that uses electromagnetic force to move an iron rod to different positions. Often used to operate a starter motor, fuel injectors and other devices.

Spare—Fifth tire carried in trunk and used to replace a flat or damaged tire.

Spark—Igniting spark or fire caused by firing of a

spark plug.

Spark Delay Valve—A Valve that delays spark vacuum advance during rapid acceleration from idle or from speeds below 15 mph and then cuts off spark advance immediately upon deceleration.

Sparkplug—Device that conducts high voltage electrical current to the two electrodes at the end of a sparkplug, causing a spark to jump between the electrodes and thus igniting the air/fuel mixture.

Speedometer—Dashboard gauge that indicates the number of miles per hour a car is traveling. The measurement is taken by a sending unit often in a transmission or driveshaft.

Spindle—Short axle extending from a movable front wheel assembly.

Spoiler—*(see air dam)*

Springs—Devices used to suspend a car body from the frame and axles. Most cars use leaf springs in the rear and coil springs in the front.

Stalling—When the engine stops running due to a lack of fuel, air, or electric current.

Starter Motor—Small, high-speed electric motor which rotates an engine enough to start and run on its own.

Starter Switch—A key is used to turn a starter switch or ignition switch which activates a starter motor via a starter solenoid.

Starving—An overly lean carburetor mixture, too much air and not enough fuel (see lean).

Steering—Series of devices that allow a driver to control the direction of the two front wheels by turning the steering wheel in the car.

Seizing—When the pistons and cylinder walls become so hot they expand and the pistons can no longer move up and down.

Stroke—The distance travelled by a piston, from its highest to lowest point in a cylinder (see bore).

Strut—Type of shock absorber also called a MacPherson strut. This suspension part uses an interior shock absorber surrounded by a large coil spring. These space saving devices appear on virtually all front wheel drive cars.

Supercharger—Device that increases air pressure in an intake manifold to pack the cylinders with additional fuel. A supercharger is like a turbocharger but uses a belt-driven air compressor instead of an exhaust gas driven turbine.

Surging—Unpredictably changing speed of an engine caused by an improper injection of gasoline by a carburetor or fuel injector.

Sun Gear—*(see planetary gear)*

Suspension—System of springs and shock absorbers used to connect but insulate a car body from a frame, engine, and wheel assemblies.

Synchromesh—System of special gears in a manual transmission that allows a driver to downshift (4th to 3rd to 2nd to lst) without grinding the gears.

T

Tachometer—Instrument used to measure the number of revolutions (rpm's) produced by an engine.

Tail Pipe—Part of the exhaust system that carries exhaust from a muffler to the rear of a car.

Tappet—Cylindrical shaped connecting device used between a push rod and a camshaft lobe.

Temperature Compensation—Device that changes operating conditions as the temperature changes.

Terminal—Connection or junction in an electrical circuit.

Thermactor System—Emission control system, recirculating fumes for reburning.

Thermostat—Device used to maintain constant temperature in a cooling system and air conditioning units.

Thermostatic Arm—Small metal arm, often used in sensors, that changes angles as temperature changes.

Throttle—Device in a carburetor (often called a butterfly valve) that controls an air/fuel mixture and air flow from a carburetor to an intake manifold.

Throw-Out Bearing—Part of a clutch system on a standard transmission that eases the forces when a clutch plate contacts the spinning crankshaft. Also called a release bearing.

Tie Rod—Metal rod that connects two parts together so that they can pivot, such as the steering gear and the front wheels.

Timing—Relationship between a crankshaft, camshaft, valves, piston and the exact time a sparkplug fires.

Timing Marks—Marks on a crankshaft pulley and an engine block that are used in adjusting the timing of an engine.

Timing Light—Tool used when tuning an engine. This flashing light illuminates the timing marks on a running engine to allow accurate adjustment of the timing of sparkplug firings.

Tires—Rubber covers for the road wheels that provide good traction.

> **Belted Bias**—Method of tire construction where an additional layer of tread is placed at an angle to the basic layer.
>
> **Bias Ply**—The standard method of tire construction with crisscrossing plies.
>
> **Radial Ply**—Similar to belted bias tires but with an additional belt running completely around a tire.
>
> **Steel belted**—use of woven steel belts as some of the tire plies.
>
> **Tubes and Tubeless**—In the past, tires had inner tubes inside to hold the pressurized air. Tires are now often sealed to a rim.

Tolerance—Clearance or variation in size that a part can tolerate before its function is affected.

Top Dead Center (TDC)—Position of the pistons relative to the crankshaft. When the number one cylinder is exactly at the top of its firing stroke.

Torque—Twisting force on a shaft measured in foot pounds(lbs. ft) The rotating ability of an engine is measured in foot pounds, as opposed to pushing or pulling power measured in horsepower.

Torque Converter—A fluid clutch used with an

automatic transmission.

Transaxle—Combination transmission and differential used on front wheel drive cars.

Transmission—Device that uses various gears and shafts to transform the usable power generated by an engine into particular functions such as different forward speeds, reverse and neutral.

Tune-Up—Maintenance operations performed periodically to restore engine performance. Often involves changing sparkplugs, adjusting ignition points, valves, sparkplug gaps, engine timing and the air/fuel mixture. There is no standard definition of a tune-up to aid consumers.

Turbocharger—Force from exhaust gases is used to turn an impeller (compressor) that packs a denser, more powerful air/fuel mixture into cylinders.

Turning Radius—Size of the circle created when a car is driven with the steering wheel "locked" hard to one side.

Turn Signals—Warning lights that blink to indicate the direction of a turn.

U

Understeer—Tendency of a front engine car to "plow" into a corner. If an understeering car goes into a corner too fast, it will slide sideways while an oversteering car will begin to spin around, back first.

Universal Joints—Commonly called U-joints, these movable joints are attached to either end of a driveshaft and connect to a transmission and differential.

V

Vacuum—Describes a condition where pressure is less than atmospheric pressure.

Vacuum Advance—Advances ignition timing based on engine load conditions. This is achieved by using engine intake manifold vacuum to operate and slightly adjust a distributor.

Vacuum Regulator—Provides constant vacuum output when vehicle is at idle.

Valve—Round metal door leading to a combustion chamber. The purpose is to open and close at the proper times so that air/fuel mixture can be taken in and exhaust can be expelled.

Valve Cover(s)—Metal covers that seal and protect a valve assembly.

Valve Job—Adjusting the amount the valves open and close, grinding and cleaning worn or carbon covered valves, or replacing bent or completely worn valves.

Vapor—Gaseous state (as opposed to liquid) of any substance.

Vapor Lock—Fuel line problem that can occur during hot conditions where the fuel heats and vaporizes. The vapor cannot be pumped so a functional block is created.

V-belt—(*see drive belt*)

Viscosity—Measure of thickness or thinness of a liquid, usually used when referring to the thickness of engine oil and grease.

Volt—Unit of measurement of electrical pressure.

Voltage Regulator—Electrical device that monitors and adjusts the voltage output of an alternator and the charging of a battery.

Volume—Amount of space occupied within a chamber or receptacle.

VTEC—Variable valve timing and electronic lift control system using cone shaped lobes that move back and forth while rotating giving an added dimension of control to a valve system as a function of engine speed.

W

Wandering—Tendency of a car to drift from its straight ahead or aimed direction, often the result of front end misalignment or improperly inflated front tires.

Water Jackets—Passages and spaces within an engine through which coolant circulates. These jackets surround the cylinders, where the greatest amount of heat can be absorbed.

Water Pump—Device mounted on the upper front of an engine block, driven by a belt from a crankshaft that circulates coolant through a cooling system.

Wheel—Combination of the rubber tire and metal rim which a tire is mounted around.

Wheel assemblies—Steel discs and drums mounted on the ends of axles and onto which the tires are mounted. Parts include hub,wheel bearings, brakes, suspension, and steering components.

Wheelbase—Distance between the centers of the two front (or rear) tires or axles of a vehicle.

Wheel Balancing—Process of adding lead weights to a wheel (tire and rim) to create a perfectly smooth and even rotation of the wheel.

Wheel Bearings—Wear resistant, grease filled metal rollers that surround an axle.

Wheel Cylinders—Hydraulic receptacles at each wheel that hold brake fluid and when expanded by pedal pressure, transfer force to friction pads.

Windshield—Safety glass used to protect drivers and passengers from wind and weather, and to provide maximum forward visibility.

Windshield Washer—System by which water and cleaning solvent is pumped from an under hood container (usually plastic) onto the windshield so that wiper action can clean a windshield.

Windshield Wipers—Metal arms and rubber blades that sweep back and forth across a windshield to give visibility in rain and snow. The wipers are driven by a small electric motor beneath the windshield and under the dash.

Wrist Pin—A steel cylinder that connects a piston with a connecting rod. Also called a piston pin.

Z

Zerk Fitting—Small metal ball and passageway usedto attach a grease gun when injecting grease into ball joints, steering gear, and other suspension parts. This fitting is sometimes called a grease nipple.

INDEX

Address Orders and Inquires to:

Black Apple Press
1609 Fern Place
Vallejo, CA 94590
call (707) 246-3803

Fax: (707) 557-2291
www.howcarswork.com